EDITOR: Maryanne Blacker

FOOD EDITOR: Pamela Clark

DESIGN DIRECTOR: Neil Carlyle

. . .

DESIGNER: Lisa Rowell

SUB EDITOR: Mary-Anne Danaher

. . .

DEPUTY FOOD EDITOR: Barbara Northwood

ASSISTANT FOOD EDITOR: Jan Castorina

ASSOCIATE FOOD EDITOR: Enid Morrison

CHIEF HOME ECONOMIST: Karen Green

HOME ECONOMISTS: Jon Allen, Jane Ash, Sue Hipwell, Louise Patniotis, Tania Thompson, Belinda Warn, Kathy Wharton,

EDITORIAL ASSISTANT: Denise Prentice

KITCHEN ASSISTANT: Amy Wong

. . .

FOOD STYLISTS: Jacqui Hing, Carolyn Fienberg, Rosemary Ingram, Michelle Gorry

PHOTOGRAPHERS: Paul Clarke, Robert Doran, Justine Kerrigan, Ashley Mackevicius, Lawrence Markham, Andre Martin, Georgia Moxham

. . .

HOME LIBRARY STAFF:

ASSISTANT EDITOR: Judy Newman

ART DIRECTOR: Robbylee Phelan

CADET ARTIST: Louise McGeachie

SECRETARY: Wendy Moore

. . .

PUBLISHER: Richard Walsh

DEPUTY PUBLISHER: Graham Lawrence

. . .

Produced by The Australian Women's Weekly Home Library. Typeset by Photoset Computer Service Pty Ltd, and Letter Perfect, Sydney. Printed by Dai Nippon Co Ltd, Tokyo, Japan. Published by Australian Consolidated Press, 54 Park Street Sydney. Distributed by Network Distribution Company, 54 Park Street Sydney. Distributed in the U.K. by Australian Consolidated Press (UK)Ltd (0604) 760 456. Distributed in Canada by Whitecap Books Ltd (604) 980 9852. Distributed in South Africa by Intermag (011) 493 3200.

. . .

© A C P 1991 (Reprint)

. . .

Basic Cookbook.
Includes index
ISBN 0 949128 29 5

1. Cookery. I. Title: Australian Women's Weekly. (Series : Australian Women's Weekly Home Library)

641.5

. . .

OUR COVER: Marshmallow Pavlova, page 100. China from Villeroy & Boch.
OPPOSITE: Fresh Tomato Soup, page 73.
Background: Metro Marble.

The BASIC COOKBOOK

In this book, we have gone right back to basics, taking you step-by-step through recipes and methods that quickly build a wide range of cooking skills. There is also a comprehensive picture guide at the back of the book with many helpful tips and techniques. We have not used salt and pepper in our cooking, allowing you to season food to suit your own requirements. Many recipes are designed to serve two people, but ingredients can be doubled to serve four or six. We want you to enjoy cooking as much as we do and, with this book, to have delicious results from your first attempt.

Pamela Clark

FOOD EDITOR

2	BREAKFAST & EGGS	75	PASTA
10	SEAFOOD	79	RICE
17	BEEF & VEAL	82	PASTRY
31	PORK	88	BATTERS
38	LAMB	90	CUSTARDS
50	CHICKEN	95	DESSERTS
63	RABBIT	105	BAKING
64	SALADS	120	GLOSSARY
71	SOUPS	127	INDEX

BRITISH & NORTH AMERICAN READERS: Please note that conversion charts for cup and spoon measurements and oven temperatures are on page 125.

BREAKFAST & EGGS

Eggs enrich so many good things we like to eat and are probably the most versatile, essential ingredient you will use. Just one egg is a power package for breakfast or a sustaining snack. Eggs also team perfectly with other flavours in tempting meals, delicious cakes, desserts and more. We show you the secret of preparing basic egg dishes and have concentrated on eggs for breakfast and snacks. Another great breakfast favourite will be our own muesli, based on today's ideas for a healthy start to the day. It is sustaining because of the complex carbohydrate and fibre content, and nourishing, as well. The compote is a delicious way to eat energy-giving dried fruit with its sweet-tart flavours. Serve the compote hot or cold as an accompaniment to muesli or other cereal or just by itself with yoghurt or cream.

MUESLI

The original muesli recipe consisted of soaked rolled oats, grated apple and yoghurt, and was made famous by Dr Bircher-Brenner, of Switzerland.

The muesli we know today is dry, and we add hot or cold milk, cream or yoghurt to make it as soft as we like.

With its range of different cereal grains, seeds, nuts and fruits, this muesli is a complete meal, providing lots of complex carbohydrate, dietary fibre (including the valuable soluble fibre in oats), plus minerals, vitamins and some protein.

We have given you weights as well as cup amounts in this recipe to help you when buying the ingredients.

If you have to buy more than you need of any ingredient, it will keep well if stored in an airtight container in the refrigerator. Or you might like to make a larger quantity and give some away.

The dried fruit we have chosen can be substituted with any other combination of dried fruit of your choice. This fruit will sweeten the muesli but, if you prefer it sweeter, simply add sugar, honey or artificial sweetener to suit your taste or diet.

Nuts are high in kilojoules but are nutritious; you can leave them out or substitute the nuts we have suggested with your favourite nuts. Peanuts and cashews are legumes, not nuts, but can also be used.

If you prefer toasted muesli, it is necessary to add oil or butter or a combination of both to brown the ingredients during toasting.

Do not add the fruit to the mixture until after it is toasted or the fruit could burn and become bitter.

HEALTHY HIGH-FIBRE MUESLI

Muesli will keep for several months in airtight container in refrigerator. Muesli can be frozen, preferably in several batches, for 3 months.

½ cup (50g) coconut
2 tablespoons (30g) sesame seeds
2 cups (185g) rolled oats
1 cup (140g) rolled rice
1 cup (100g) rolled triticale
½ cup (80g) oat bran
½ cup (60g) wheatgerm
2 tablespoons (40g) sunflower
   seed kernels
2 tablespoons (40g) pepitas
   (pumpkin seed kernels)
½ cup (70g) pecans or walnuts,
   chopped
½ cup (80g) hazelnuts, chopped
¾ cup (100g) dried apricots
½ cup (45g) dried apples
½ cup (90g) sultanas

1. Combine coconut and sesame seeds in frying pan, stir constantly over medium heat until both ingredients are lightly browned. Place into large bowl, mix in rolled oats, rice and triticale, then oat bran, wheatgerm, sunflower kernels, pepitas and nuts.

2. Chop apricots and apples into small pieces with scissors, stir into oat mixture with sultanas. Transfer mixture to airtight container.

Makes about 9 cups (1¼kg).

¼ cup (about 30g) muesli contains about 550 kilojoules (130 calories).

TOASTED MUESLI

Heat 60g butter and 2 tablespoons oil in baking dish, add mixture, stir well in butter and oil. Bake, uncovered, in moderate oven for 10 minutes.

Remove muesli from oven, stir well. Return to oven, bake further 50 minutes, stirring every 10 minutes, or until browned. Remove from oven, stir in fruit. Cool to room temperature before transferring to storage jar.

MICROWAVE COOKING

Muesli will also toast well in a microwave oven. Heat 60g butter and 2 tablespoons oil in large microwave-proof bowl or microwave-proof dish on HIGH for 1 minute.

Add remaining ingredients (except the fruit), microwave on HIGH for about 12 minutes or until well browned; stir every 3 minutes during cooking time so mixture will toast evenly. Stir in fruit, cool to room temperature before transferring to storage jar or airtight container.

LEFT: Healthy High-Fibre Muesli.

DRIED FRUIT COMPOTE

The good flavours of dried fruit can be enjoyed as a breakfast or brunch dish. There are many varieties to choose from, and a fruit salad of these makes a refreshing compote when the fruit is cooked in a flavoured syrup.

FRUIT COMPOTE IN LEMON GINGER SYRUP

Compote can be made a week ahead; keep, covered, in refrigerator. It is delicious served with yoghurt or cream, or as an accompaniment to cereal. We used packaged fruit salad but any dried fruit of your choice is suitable. Recipe unsuitable to freeze or microwave.

1¼ cups water
½ teaspoon grated fresh ginger
1 teaspoon grated lemon rind
1 tablespoon lemon juice
⅓ cup sugar
250g dried fruit salad

Combine water, ginger, lemon rind and juice and sugar in large saucepan. Stir constantly over medium heat, without boiling, until sugar is dissolved. Increase heat, bring to boil, add dried fruit, reduce heat, simmer, uncovered, for about 20 minutes or until fruit is plump; stir occasionally. Remove pan from heat, cool to room temperature, cover, refrigerate.

Serves 4.

BELOW: Fruit Compote in Lemon Ginger Syrup.

BOILED EGGS

Boiled eggs are a great favourite for breakfast, and we tell you how to cook the popular 3-minute egg, where the white is set and the yolk soft. For a little variety, we have given you a tasty curry sauce to transform boiled eggs into a delicious snack with toast or a main course with boiled rice.

1. Choose saucepan to suit the number of eggs you are boiling: 1 egg in small saucepan, up to 4 eggs in medium saucepan; more eggs in large saucepan (there should be enough room to move eggs around). Add enough cold water to cover eggs, stir constantly with wooden spoon over high heat until water boils; this will centralise each yolk. Boil, uncovered, until yolks are as soft or as firm as you like. As a guide, 3 minutes will give you set egg white and soft yolk. After 5 minutes, the yolk will be set.

2. Place saucepan of eggs under cold running water for about 1 minute or until eggs are cool enough to handle. To peel eggs, crack shells gently and leave eggs immersed in cold water for at least 5 minutes or until cold. This will stop a dark ring forming around each yolk. Remove shells, starting from broad end. Wash eggs, pat dry with absorbent paper.

CURRIED EGGS

Eggs and sauce can be prepared up to a day ahead; keep, covered, in refrigerator. Recipe unsuitable to freeze or microwave.

3 tablespoons oil
8 hard-boiled eggs
1 teaspoon black mustard seeds
1 clove garlic, crushed
1 teaspoon grated fresh ginger
1 small onion, finely sliced
1 teaspoon ground cumin
2 tablespoons curry powder

½ teaspoon ground cardamom
425g can tomatoes
1 teaspoon sugar
½ cup water

1. Heat oil in medium saucepan over medium heat, add eggs, stir occasionally and gently until eggs are well-browned all over; drain on absorbent paper. At this stage, eggs will have a crusty surface.

2. Discard oil in saucepan except for about 1 tablespoon. Reheat this oil in saucepan. Add mustard seeds, cover,

cook over high heat for about 30 seconds or until seeds begin to crack. Stir in garlic, ginger and onion; cook, stirring constantly, until onion is soft. Stir in cumin, curry powder, cardamom, undrained crushed tomatoes, sugar and water. Bring sauce to boil, add eggs, reduce heat, cover, simmer for 5 minutes.

Serves 4.

ABOVE: Curried Eggs.

Table: Keyhole Furniture

5

POACHED EGG

It's very personal the way you like your egg poached; it can be soft or hard or somewhere in between. Always choose the freshest available eggs for poaching. The white of a stale egg is watery and will not hold its shape during poaching. Always use a frying pan so you can reach the egg easily with an egg slide: a saucepan is too deep to remove the egg undamaged.

THE SIMPLEST WAY

The simplest way is to use an egg ring, available in hardware stores and supermarkets. The ring forms a neat round egg without any worry and is easy to handle.

Lift the cooked egg from the pan with an egg slide, place onto hot buttered toast, muffin or crumpet, etc.
1. Put a little butter or oil on your index finger and grease inside egg ring or spray lightly with non-stick spray. Place about 1cm water in frying pan so egg will not be covered. Bring water to boil, reduce heat until water is barely simmering. Place ring into water, gently pour egg into ring.

2. Egg white will start to set. If egg is large, a little white may seem to puff up around top of ring. Make sure water doesn't boil or white will toughen. Now start spooning water over yolk until it is set enough to suit your taste.

It is not possible to give a time as this depends on type and size of pan, amount and heat of water, size and temperature of egg and, most important, individual preferences.

3. Carefully lift egg ring away from egg, lift egg from water with egg slide.

TOP: Poached Egg.

China: Villeroy & Boch

MICROWAVE COOKING

A microwave oven will also cook an egg very effectively; the egg has a texture similar to an egg cooked in an electric or manual poaching appliance.

Break an egg into an ordinary teacup (it is not necessary to grease the cup), prick the yolk with a fork otherwise the yolk will burst during cooking. Microwave on HIGH for about 30 seconds or until cooked as desired.

THE CLASSIC WAY

The classic way to poach an egg is to place water in the pan, stir water briskly with a wooden spoon to cause a whirlpool, then gently lower the egg from a jug or cup into the centre of the swirling water. The swirling action of the water shapes the egg neatly.

Adjust the heat so the water is barely simmering, then cook the egg covered or uncovered, as we have already outlined above.

If you cover the pan with a lid, start checking after a minute to see if the egg is done to your liking.

If you don't cover the pan, spoon the water gently over the egg until the yolk is set to suit your taste.

POACHING APPLIANCES

There are poachers available for poaching eggs, both electric and manual. Strictly speaking, these are not poachers but steamers.

The egg containers need to be greased lightly and evenly with butter or oil or a non-stick spray, unless the container has a non-stick surface.

There are also individual egg poaching containers which you simply stand in a pan with enough water to come half way up the side of the container. These poachers must always be covered with a lid to trap the steam which cooks the egg.

POACHING

Poaching is a gentle method of cooking food in simmering liquid. Food can be lowered into the simmering liquid or it can be placed in the pan then the liquid added and heated until simmering. Liquid should almost cover the food, not submerge it.

The pan may be covered or uncovered.
● **When covered**, the food is cooked by the trapped steam as well as the simmering liquid.
● **When uncovered**, the liquid can be spooned over the top of the food until it is cooked to suit your taste.

Follow individual recipes. Foods suitable for poaching: eggs, seafood, chicken, fruit.

SCRAMBLED EGGS

Scrambled eggs are simply eggs mixed with milk (or cream) and butter, then stirred gently over low heat until cooked to your personal taste. As with boiled and poached eggs, everyone likes eggs scrambled differently.

It is correct to have the eggs barely firm when cooked, and they should be creamy in texture.

You must be patient when cooking scrambled eggs; it is important to keep the heat low and even, and not to stir them too much. If they are cooked too quickly the eggs will toughen; or if they are stirred too much they will separate with a fine crumbly texture floating in a watery substance. There is nothing you can do to retrieve these mistakes; however, they are still edible even if they don't look creamy.

You need to use a heavy-based medium-sized saucepan with a base measuring about 18cm. Thin pans transfer the heat too quickly to the eggs and tend to burn the mixture. Stirring is best done with a wooden spoon, using a folding action.

Cream can be used instead of milk for a richer result; the thin pouring cream will give the best results.

We used both parsley and chives to flavour our recipe; you can use one or the other, as you prefer, or leave herbs out completely.

Scrambled eggs should be prepared just before they are required as they can't be reheated successfully.

BELOW: Herbed Scrambled Eggs.

China: Incorporated Agencies

HERBED SCRAMBLED EGGS

4 eggs
⅓ cup milk
**1 tablespoon finely chopped
    fresh parsley**
**1 tablespoon finely chopped
    fresh chives**
1 teaspoon butter

1. Lightly beat eggs in small bowl with whisk, whisk in milk and herbs.

2. Melt butter in medium saucepan over heat, add egg mixture; heat should be gentle. When mixture begins to set on base of pan, gently fold egg mixture over with wooden spoon so uncooked mixture runs to base of pan. Do not beat or stir vigorously or the texture will be crumbly. Continue to cook and fold gently until eggs are still creamy and slightly firm.

Serves 2.

MICROWAVE COOKING

Place butter into shallow dish; we used a pie plate. Melt on HIGH for about 15 seconds. Add egg mixture, cook on HIGH for about 3 minutes or until barely firm. Stir egg mixture with wooden spoon twice during cooking time, using a gentle folding action.

FRIED EGG

Always choose the freshest egg available so the white will set in a good shape when cooked; a stale egg will result in a watery white when cooked.

Use a heavy-based frying pan; the size doesn't matter. Gentle cooking is the secret; use a little butter or oil in the pan or a pan sprayed with non-stick spray. You can also use a pan with a non-stick surface.

If you want a nice round egg, use an egg ring; grease it first with a little butter or oil on your index finger or use a non-stick spray.

Butter should be hot but not browned when you put in the egg; if the butter is too hot the egg will burn around the edge and underneath before the centre is cooked.

Some people prefer a fried egg which is a little crispy on the base. To attain this, increase the heat carefully until the white is as crisp as you like.

You should serve the egg immediately it is cooked as a fried egg cannot be reheated successfully.

FRIED EGG BURGER

A fried egg with just the texture you like makes a tempting, hearty snack on a roll stacked with cheese and salad. This recipe is unsuitable to freeze or microwave.

30g butter or 1 tablespoon oil
1 small onion, thickly sliced
1 hamburger roll
1 egg
lettuce
tomato slices
alfalfa sprouts
processed cheese slice

1. Melt butter in frying pan. Separate onion slices into rings, add to pan, stir constantly over medium heat with

wooden spoon for about 1 minute or until onion is soft. Remove onion from pan, drain onion on absorbent paper. Do not discard butter in pan. Split roll in half; toast cut sides under hot griller.

TOP: Fried Egg Burger.

China: Wedgwood

2. Reheat butter in pan; it should be hot but not browned. Crack egg into cup, carefully pour egg into pan. Use egg slide to splash a little of the butter over yolk until egg is as firm as you like it. Or if you want egg cooked on both sides, now is the time to turn it over.

3. Using egg slide and spatula, quickly turn egg over, cook further 1 minute or until egg is as firm as you like. Assemble egg burger with the remaining ingredients.
Makes 1.

FRENCH OMELETTE

Omelettes come in many different types; we show you how to make a basic French omelette. The eggs are beaten lightly then cooked quickly over a fairly high heat; the omelette can be eaten with or without filling.

It is important to work quickly or the egg mixture in contact with the base and side of the pan will cook too much and will brown and toughen; the finished omelette should be only lightly browned underneath.

We used a fairly heavy aluminium omelette pan with a base measuring around 20cm.

Some cooks prefer to keep a pan especially for omelettes; in this case, washing is unnecessary. Simply wipe out the pan properly with a pad of absorbent paper. Put the pan away carefully to avoid scratching the surface in any way.

The depth of the omelette pan doesn't really matter, although a shallow pan makes the omelette easier to remove by slipping the omelette from the pan to the plate.

If using an aluminium pan it should be "seasoned" by heating the pan, then "polishing" it vigorously with about a tablespoon of coarse cooking salt. A pad of absorbent paper makes an ideal polisher.

To season a copper pan, place a knob of butter into the pan and heat the pan until the butter burns. Use a pad of absorbent paper to wipe pan.

FRENCH OMELETTE WITH HAM AND CHEESE

2 eggs
1 tablespoon water
2 teaspoons butter
1 medium tomato
1 slice ham
¼ cup grated tasty cheese
1 tablespoon chopped fresh chives

1. Break eggs into medium bowl, add water, use fork or whisk to mix only until yolks and whites are blended. Heat pan over high heat for about 1 minute. Add butter to pan; it should sizzle and foam immediately if pan is hot enough; do not allow butter to brown. Tip pan so butter covers base and halfway up side evenly.

Pour egg mixture into hot pan; it should begin to set around edge of pan almost immediately. Use wooden spoon to pull edge of omelette away from side of pan, allowing running mixture to reach hot pan and cook. Omelette is cooked when egg mixture no longer runs freely, but top still looks creamy. Omelette should be only lightly browned underneath.

2. Spoon filling over half the omelette, opposite handle, as shown; this makes it easier to slide omelette onto plate when cooked. Use egg slide to help fold omelette in half, covering filling, and slide onto serving plate; serve omelette immediately.

Filling: Cut tomato in half, remove seeds (see glossary), cut flesh into strips. Cut ham into strips. Combine

tomato and ham in bowl with cheese and chives, mix lightly.

Serves 1.

BELOW: French Omelette.

China: Villeroy & Boch

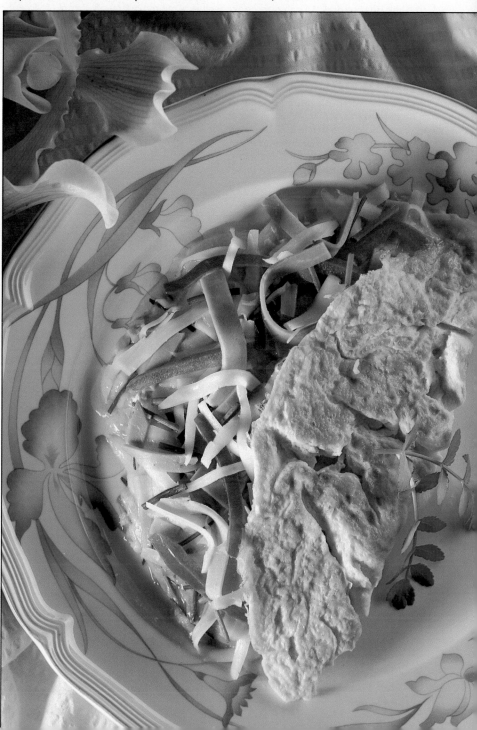

SEAFOOD

There is a wealth of wonderful seafood to enjoy, and we show you how to make five tempting dishes, all top favourites and very simple to prepare. With our recipes, you can master the techniques of pan-frying, deep-frying, the popular prawn cocktail, versatile mornay sauce and tender oven-baked fish cutlets. Grilled fish and other types of seafood are terrific for dieters; the types suitable are: lobster, crabs, bream, gemfish, jewfish (mulloway), leatherjacket, John dory, ling, mullet, kingfish, perch, sardines (pilchards), redfish, prawns, scallops, snapper, tailor and whiting. Always choose the freshest seafood and remember that cooking times are usually quite short so it is best not to leave seafood to cook unattended. All seafood cooks well in a microwave oven; simply follow the maker's instructions.

PRAWN COCKTAIL

Prawns nestling on lettuce, served with lemon and the traditional sauce, make an entrée that is a firm favourite with Australians. The quantity of prawns in our recipe can be reduced and crab and/or oysters can be used, too. Always choose the freshest seafood available.

The addition of grapefruit and avocado makes our cocktail a little more interesting, in colour, texture and taste.

Use a commercial or home-made mayonnaise as the base for the sauce.

PRAWN, AVOCADO AND GRAPEFRUIT COCKTAIL

Sauce for cocktail can be prepared up to a week ahead; keep, covered, in refrigerator until required. Recipe unsuitable to freeze.

400g cooked king prawns
1 small grapefruit
lettuce leaves
½ medium avocado, chopped
lemon slices
COCKTAIL SAUCE
½ cup mayonnaise
2½ tablespoons tomato sauce
¼ teaspoon Worcestershire sauce
¼ teaspoon chilli sauce

1. Pinch heads from bodies of prawns. Pinch tail section away, then peel shell

away from centre part of body. If you want to keep tails intact, leave tail and next section of shell in place, then pull away centre shell, as shown.
2. Remove back veins by pulling veins from head end towards tail end.

3. Using sharp knife, cut top and bottom from grapefruit, cut away skin and white pith.

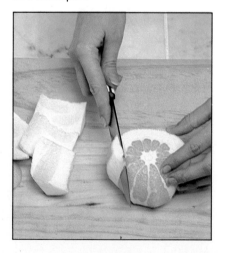

4. Cut between membranes of each grapefruit segment. Line serving dishes with lettuce leaves, place prawns, grapefruit and avocado into dishes, spoon cocktail sauce over prawn mixture. Garnish with prawns (with tails intact), lemon and a sprig of dill or parsley, if desired.

Cocktail Sauce: Combine mayonnaise and sauces in small bowl, mix well.
Serves 2.

RIGHT: Prawn, Avocado and Grapefruit Cocktail.

Glass: Dansab; background: Abet Laminati

PAN-FRYING FISH

Pan-frying fish is a tasty alternative to grilling. You can use 30g butter instead of the 2 tablespoons oil in our recipe, or a combination of 15g butter and 1 tablespoon oil. Butter gives a distinct flavour to fish when pan-fried but it burns easily. The addition of oil helps prevent burning.

Small whole fish, cutlets, fillets and steaks can be pan-fried.

We used bream fillets for this recipe; other fish suitable for pan-frying include flathead, garfish, gemfish, leatherjacket, John dory, mirror dory, jewfish (mulloway), kingfish, perch, redfish, trevally and whiting.

It is difficult to give a cooking time for this method because the type of pan, the heat, and the size and type of fish will all affect the cooking time.

Test fish by gently piercing with a fork; fish should flake easily when ready to serve. If over-cooked it will be tough, dry and not so tasty.

Tartare sauce, a traditional accompaniment for fish, can be bought ready-made but is quick and easy to make at home. Use commercial or home-made mayonnaise as the base for the sauce.

PAN-FRIED FISH WITH TARTARE SAUCE

We used bream fillets in this recipe. Tartare sauce can be prepared up to a week ahead; keep, covered, in refrigerator. Recipe unsuitable to freeze or microwave.

2 white fish fillets
coarse cooking salt
1 tablespoon plain flour
2 tablespoons oil
TARTARE SAUCE
½ cup mayonnaise
1 large gherkin, finely chopped
1 tablespoon drained capers, chopped
2 teaspoons chopped fresh parsley
½ teaspoon lemon juice
¼ teaspoon Worcestershire sauce
1. Remove skin from fillets by placing fillets skin-side-down onto chopping board. Dip fingers into a little salt; this

makes it easier for you to hold and handle the fish. Hold skin at tail firmly. Using sharp knife held at an angle, use a "press and push" action carefully to separate flesh from skin.

2. Dust fillets lightly with flour. Heat oil in large, shallow, heavy-based frying pan, place fillets skinned-side-up in the hot oil. Cook over medium heat until fillets are lightly browned underneath. Use egg slide to turn fillets over carefully, continue to cook over medium heat until fish flakes easily when tested with a fork. Serve immediately with tartare sauce.
Tartare Sauce: Place mayonnaise in small bowl, add other ingredients; mix well together.

ABOVE: Pan-Fried Fish with Tartare Sauce.

Table: Colonial Castings

FISH BAKED IN FOIL

Fish wrapped in foil is ideal for baking in the oven and for barbecuing. The fish steams to tender, flaky perfection in its own juices, and you can add a little butter and other ingredients for flavour (herbs are nice).

However, if you are on a fat-free diet, simply omit the butter and substitute a suitable vegetable for the potato chips in our picture. We used commercially prepared chips, ready for oven-baking.

Whole fish, steaks, cutlets and fillets are all good for this method of cooking. We used jewfish (mulloway) cutlets; other suitable fish include bream, flathead, gemfish, ling, mullet, perch, snapper, tailor and whiting.

Use a good-quality foil or a double thickness of the thinner variety and wrap foil as described to enclose the fish completely.

Foil makes serving easier, too, as each person has an individual parcel. Serve the fish cutlets with a squeeze of lemon or lime juice.

OVEN-BAKED FISH CUTLETS

This recipe is not suitable to freeze or microwave.

2 x 200g white fish cutlets
30g butter
2 tablespoons lime or lemon juice
black pepper
1. Place each piece of fish onto a piece of foil larger than the fish, pleat ends of foil to partially enclose fish.

2. Divide butter between fish, pour juice over fish; grind a little black pepper over fish.

3. Pleat foil firmly over fish to enclose completely. Place onto oven tray, bake in moderate oven for about 25 minutes or until fish flakes easily when tested with a fork. Unwrap partially to serve.
Serves 2.

BELOW: Oven-Baked Fish Cutlets.

Plate: Corso de Fiori

DEEP-FRYING

Deep-frying is an efficient method of cooking if it is done correctly. It is usually a quick method used for foods that require minimum cooking time, such as patties, croquettes, seafood, chicken, sweetbread and brains, etc, and fruit. Food usually has a coating such as batter or crumbs to protect it.

It is important to use a wide-topped, deep frying pan, preferably with a heavy base. The pan we used is about 25cm diameter and about 10cm deep. Never cover the frying pan.

A frying basket makes it easy to lift the food in and out of the oil without damage to the food.

There are thermostatically controlled deep fryers available; always follow the manufacturer's instructions when using these.

OIL FOR FRYING

We use a good-quality all-purpose oil for frying. There are many types available, you should read labels to check suitability. There are also solid types of shortening available for frying.

The pan should be a tiny bit more than half-full of oil; excessive oil is not only wasteful but can be dangerous.

Heat the oil, uncovered, on the highest temperature. It doesn't take long, so don't leave the pan unattended because the oil will burn and could ignite if over-heated.

When the oil is hot enough for deep-frying it will be perfectly still and there will be a slight haze (not smoke) coming from the surface. Drop a cube of bread into the oil if you are in doubt; it should sink to the bottom, rise to the surface almost immediately and turn golden brown.

The most accurate way to judge if the oil is at the correct temperature is to use a thermometer; these are available at hardware and kitchen stores (see glossary for how to handle a thermometer). The oil will be ready for most food at 190 degrees Celsius (375 degrees Fahrenheit).

After the oil has been used, cool it to room temperature, strain well and pour back into the bottle or jar; keep it in the refrigerator. If the oil has bits and pieces in it from frying, line the strainer with absorbent paper.

Because oil absorbs flavours, you will find that oil used for cooking savoury food is best kept for use with other savoury food; fresh oil should be used to cook sweet food.

COOKING SALMON PATTIES

Salmon patties are great favourites and are delicious eaten hot or cold. To cook the patties so they look wonderful and don't fall apart, it is necessary to deep-fry them.

Use any type of salmon you like. It must be drained very well because excess moisture can cause the patties to break up and spatter during frying. Remove any large bones which won't mash with a fork and discard dark skin. Tuna can be used instead of salmon, if you prefer.

Potatoes must be mashed finely with a fork or masher. It is important that they are drained well before mashing; do not add any butter, milk, cream or water; moisture will make the patties too soft. Left-over potatoes can be used again provided you added nothing to them when mashing.

Do not process potatoes in a food processor because they will break down and turn gluey.

When following our recipe, be sure the pepper and celery are chopped finely; big chunks will cause the patties to break up.

Crumbs can be any type of packaged crumbs or crumbs you have made yourself by processing stale bread until fine or rubbing stale bread through a sieve. Use either or a combination of both.

Make the patties as large or as small as you like. They make great savouries to have with drinks when rolled into balls about 3cm in diameter.

Remember, the cooking and reheating times will be shorter for these tidbits.

REHEATING

Patties can be fried and reheated when required, although they are not quite as good as when fried and served immediately. The best way to reheat them from refrigerator temperature is to place them about 1cm apart on a flat oven tray. Cover with foil, then slash holes in the foil to allow steam to escape. Bake in a moderate oven for about 15 minutes or until hot.

SALMON PATTIES

Patties can be prepared for frying up to a day ahead; keep, covered, in refrigerator. Recipe unsuitable to freeze or microwave.

5 medium (500g) potatoes
440g can salmon
1 stick celery, finely chopped
1 small onion, grated
1 small red pepper, finely chopped
1 tablespoon chopped fresh parsley
1 teaspoon grated lemon rind
1 tablespoon lemon juice
½ cup plain flour, approximately
1 egg, lightly beaten
2 tablespoons milk
1 cup packaged breadcrumbs, approximately
1 cup stale breadcrumbs, approximately
oil for deep frying

1. Boil, steam or microwave potatoes until tender; drain well, place in medium bowl, mash with fork or potato masher until smooth. Drain salmon well, remove skin and bones, add to bowl, mash with fork, add celery, onion, pepper, parsley and lemon rind and juice, mix well with fork. Cover, refrigerate for 30 minutes to make mixture easier to handle.

2. Divide salmon mixture evenly into 8 portions; a simple way is to divide mixture into 8 wedges, see picture. Shape each portion into patty, dust with flour, shake away excess flour. Brush patties with combined egg and milk, toss in combined breadcrumbs; reshape if necessary while patting on the breadcrumbs.

3. Place patties into frying basket, leaving about 1cm between each patty. Lower gently into hot oil, deep-fry for about 2 minutes or until golden brown, Drain on absorbent paper. Serve with lemon to squeeze over patties.
Makes 8.

RIGHT: Salmon Patties.

MORNAY SAUCE

When you add cheese to a white sauce it becomes mornay sauce and is useful as a basis for many tasty dishes. Hard-boiled eggs, salmon, smoked fish, cooked chicken, asparagus and many different vegetables are some of the ingredients you can add to this kind of sauce. Here we have used it with tuna.

TUNA MORNAY

Mornay can be prepared up to the stage of baking a day before required; keep, covered, in refrigerator. All milk can be used instead of the cream; we added cream for a little extra richness. Recipe unsuitable to freeze.

30g butter
1 medium onion, finely chopped
1 stick celery, finely chopped
1 tablespoon plain flour
¾ cup milk
½ cup cream
⅓ cup grated tasty cheese
130g can corn niblets, drained
185g can tuna, drained
½ cup stale breadcrumbs
¼ cup grated tasty cheese, extra

1. Melt butter in medium saucepan, add onion and celery, stir constantly over medium heat for about 3 minutes or until onion is soft. Add flour, stir constantly over medium heat for 1 minute or until mixture is bubbly. Gradually stir in combined milk and cream; stir constantly over high heat until mixture boils and thickens.

2. Remove from heat, add cheese, corn and tuna, stir gently until cheese is melted. Spoon the mixture into 2 ovenproof dishes. Sprinkle with combined breadcrumbs and extra cheese. Bake in moderate oven for about 15 minutes or until mornay is heated through.

Serves 2.

MICROWAVE COOKING

Combine butter, onion and celery in microwave-proof dish, cook on HIGH for about 3 minutes or until onion is soft. Stir in flour, then milk and cream, cook on HIGH for about 2 minutes or until mixture boils and thickens; stir twice during cooking time.

Stir in cheese, corn and tuna, sprinkle top with combined bread-crumbs and extra cheese, cook on HIGH, uncovered, for about 3 minutes or until cheese is melted.

ABOVE: Tuna Mornay.

BEEF & VEAL

Beef is one of the most satisfying and popular meats. Today, we are fortunate to have a lavish variety of cuts to use in so many tasty dishes. Australia produces the leanest beef in the world, but it is still advisable to cut off as much fat as possible, then cook the meat in the minimum amount of butter or oil. Grilled meat needs no butter or oil for cooking, but a variety of butters can be added as flavour boosters. We show you how to make beef dishes for family meals, barbecues and to serve at dinner parties; these use cuts of many types and costs to suit the occasion. Your butcher will be glad to advise you if you are in doubt about the suitability of any cut of beef for the cooking method. Veal is always leaner than beef and lighter in colour. It needs moist methods of cooking (for example, casseroles and stews) for best results, or it needs to be covered with a crumb coating to protect it during frying.

MEATLOAF

Ask the butcher for the best and leanest topside for this meatloaf. We bought lean, trimmed topside steak and minced it in a food processor.

This is a basic meatloaf recipe; you can add a variety of vegetables to change the flavour as you prefer. For example, ½ cup of cooked, frozen or canned corn, grated carrot and chopped peppers can all be added.

The addition of sausage mince will give the loaf a finer, better-cutting texture than if you used all topside mince. Cooked rice can be used in place of the breadcrumbs.

Meatloaf can be served hot as a main meal with vegetables or as a cold meal with salad. It is ideal for lunches and picnics, and makes a tasty sandwich filling.

TASTY BAKED MEATLOAF

Cooked meatloaf can be frozen for 2 months.

½ cup fresh or frozen peas
250g minced beef
500g sausage mince
1 egg
1 medium onion, finely chopped
1 teaspoon dried mixed herbs
⅓ cup packaged breadcrumbs
1. Boil, steam or microwave peas until tender; drain. Combine both minces in medium bowl, mix well with wooden spoon or your hand. Mix in egg, onion, herbs and half the breadcrumbs. Mix in

peas gently. Grease an ovenproof loaf dish or pan (base measures 14cm x 21cm), sprinkle with some of the remaining breadcrumbs. Press mixture gently into dish. Sprinkle top with remaining breadcrumbs.

2. Bake in moderate oven for about 1 hour or until the juices are clear when

a skewer is inserted into the meatloaf. Stand for 5 minutes before turning onto wire rack over a tray.

MICROWAVE COOKING

Press mixture into microwave-proof loaf dish (base measures 14cm x 21cm), cover with lid or plastic wrap, cook on HIGH for about 20 minutes. If corners of loaf cook too quickly, cover corners of dish with pieces of foil.

ABOVE: Tasty Baked Meatloaf.

Platter & wooden chest: Chelsea House Antiques

RISSOLES

Good, old-fashioned rissoles or meat patties are tasty and wholesome (the name rissole comes from a French term meaning to brown food). Use good-quality mince, or mince or process your own steak; topside steak is ideal.

Rissoles can be eaten hot or cold and are a great portable food for picnics and school lunches. The mixture can be made into 3cm balls to serve as savouries with drinks.

Rissoles and meatballs reheat well. Place in a single layer on an oven tray, cover with foil, slash holes in foil to let steam escape, reheat in moderate oven for 10 to 20 minutes or until heated through.

We used only a little butter and oil to prevent the rissoles sticking to the pan during cooking. If you use a non-stick pan, you can eliminate the oil and butter. There will be enough pan drippings from the rissoles to make the sauce.

TASTY HERBED RISSOLES WITH MUSHROOM SAUCE

Rissoles can be made a day ahead; keep, covered, in refrigerator. They can be frozen, uncooked and unfloured, for up to 2 months. Recipe unsuitable to microwave.

375g minced beef
1 small onion, finely chopped
1 small carrot, coarsely grated
1 small red pepper, finely chopped
½ teaspoon dried thyme leaves
1 clove garlic, crushed
1 egg, lightly beaten
¼ cup plain flour
15g butter
2 teaspoons oil
MUSHROOM SAUCE
2 tablespoons plain flour
2 tablespoons dry red wine
1 cup water
1 small beef stock cube, crumbled
3 green shallots, finely chopped
60g small mushrooms, sliced

1. Combine mince, onion, carrot, pepper, thyme, garlic and egg in medium bowl. Mix with wooden spoon until ingredients are well combined.

2. Divide mixture into 4 equal portions, roll into balls, flatten slightly into rissole shapes. Place flour in shallow bowl or plate, toss rissoles in flour, shake off excess flour.

3. Heat butter and oil in medium frying pan over medium heat. Add rissoles, cook for about 10 minutes on each side. Turn rissoles with egg slide several times during cooking; drain on absorbent paper.

4. Mushroom Sauce: Measure approximately 2 tablespoons of the pan drippings into small saucepan, stir in flour, stir constantly over medium heat for about 1 minute or until flour mixture browns lightly. Gradually stir in combined wine, water and stock cube, stir constantly over high heat until sauce boils and thickens.

5. Add shallots and mushrooms to sauce, simmer for 2 minutes. Place rissoles on serving plates, pour sauce over rissoles and serve with the vegetables of your choice.

Makes 4.

RIGHT: Tasty Herbed Rissoles with Mushroom Sauce.

Plate & cutlery: Casa Shopping

BEEF IN RED WINE CASSEROLE

This tasty casserole recipe can be doubled easily to serve 4 people. Mashed potatoes, rice or noodles (see glossary) would be ideal to serve with it, along with a green vegetable such as broccoli, peas or beans.

The cooking time is directly related to the cut of beef used; some cuts take longer than others to become as tender as required. We have used round steak in this recipe; other cuts which will cook in about the same time are skirt, blade and topside steak.

The dish can also be cooked on top of the stove instead of in the oven; it will take about the same cooking time.

For stove-top cooking, use a heavy-based pan with a tight-fitting lid. Bring mixture to boil, reduce heat to low, simmer, covered, for 1 hour. Check several times during cooking to make sure heat is low enough to maintain a gentle simmer. Add onions, as below, simmer until steak is tender.

BEEF IN RED WINE CASSEROLE

Casserole can be made up to 3 days ahead; keep, covered, in refrigerator. It can be frozen for up to 3 months. Recipe unsuitable to microwave.

375g round steak
3 bacon rashers
6 small onions
15g butter
2 teaspoons oil
30g butter, extra
1 clove garlic, crushed
1½ tablespoons plain flour
2 teaspoons tomato paste
¾ cup water
1 small beef stock cube, crumbled
¼ cup dry red wine

1. Trim fat from steak, cut steak into 3cm pieces. Remove rind from bacon, chop bacon into large pieces. Peel onions, leaving some of root area intact to hold onions together during the cooking time.

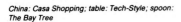

RIGHT: Beef in Red Wine Casserole.

China: Casa Shopping; table: Tech-Style; spoon: The Bay Tree

2. Heat butter and oil in frying pan until mixture is sizzling. Add half the steak in single layer, stir constantly over high heat until meat is well browned all over. Remove from pan to ovenproof dish, leaving butter mixture in pan. Cook remaining steak in the same way, add to ovenproof dish.

3. Place bacon and onions in pan, stir constantly over high heat until onions are lightly browned, remove from pan.

4. Add extra butter to pan, add garlic, cook, stirring, over low heat for 30 seconds. Add flour, cook over medium heat, stirring constantly until browned. Remove from heat, gradually stir in combined tomato paste, water, stock cube and wine: Return to heat, stir constantly over high heat until mixture boils and thickens. Pour into ovenproof dish, cover with lid or foil, bake in moderate oven for 1 hour, add onions and bacon, cover, bake further 30 minutes or until steak is tender.
Serves 2.

BEEF STROGANOFF

This dish of tender beef strips in creamy, piquant sauce originated in Russia. It makes an ideal dish for a party as it is easy to eat with a fork. The most tender cuts of beef are best; we use rump or Scotch fillet for quick cooking and tasty eating.

If making a quantity larger than our recipe, you will need to use a larger pan; a deep frying pan or electric frying pan would be ideal. The medium saucepan we suggest suits the quantity of meat we used.

It is important that the steak be sealed in the initial stages of cooking. This simply means that the pan should be very hot to sear and seal the surfaces of the steak pieces. The steak should be added gradually to the saucepan so all the pieces have a chance to be sealed. If the steak is added too quickly or if the pan is not hot enough, the steak will stew, juices will escape and the steak will be tough.

BEEF STROGANOFF

Stroganoff can be made up to a day ahead without the sour cream and tomato paste. It will freeze for up to 2 months without the mushrooms, sour cream and tomato paste. Add these after reheating steak. Recipe unsuitable to microwave.

375g rump steak, in one piece
3 teaspoons plain flour
½ teaspoon paprika
30g butter
1 small onion, finely chopped
1 small clove garlic, crushed
125g small mushrooms
2 teaspoons lemon juice
1 tablespoon dry red wine
1 tablespoon tomato paste
¾ cup sour cream
1 tablespoon chopped fresh chives

1. Wrap steak in plastic wrap, freeze for about 30 minutes or until partly frozen. Remove plastic; use sharp knife to cut steak into thin slices. Place steak into plastic bag with flour and paprika, shake until steak is well coated with flour mixture.

2. Melt butter in medium saucepan, add onion and garlic, stir constantly over medium heat for about 3 minutes or until onion is soft. Increase heat to high, add steak gradually to saucepan; stir constantly until all steak is browned all over.

3. Add mushrooms, juice and wine, stir until ingredients are combined. Reduce heat; cover, simmer over low heat for about 5 minutes or until steak is tender.

4. Stir in tomato paste and sour cream, stir constantly over heat until mixture is heated through. Serve with boiled pasta or rice (see glossary); sprinkle with chives before serving.

Serves 2.

RIGHT: Beef Stroganoff.

Bowl: Casa Shopping; fork: The Bay Tree

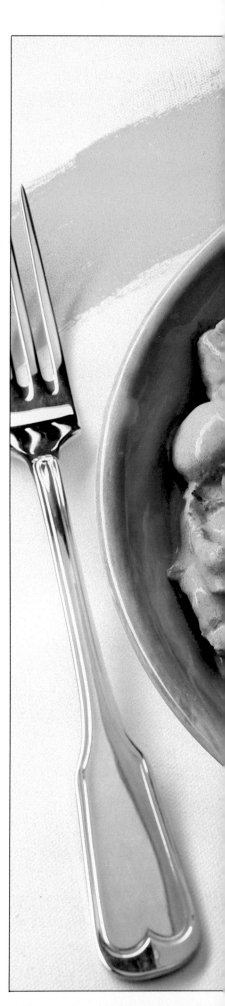

FILET MIGNON

Mignons are small pieces of steak about 3cm thick. Filet Mignon, wrapped in bacon, is a specialty of many restaurants but is so easy to make at home.

The steak must be cooked at the last minute and you do need the pan drippings to make the sauce a good colour and really tasty.

Eye fillet is the traditional cut to use for this recipe as it is the most tender, also the most expensive. However, there is no bone, hardly any fat and therefore no waste.

Ask the butcher to cut the steaks all the same size and thickness for you to make the cooking as even as possible.

FILET MIGNON WITH MUSHROOM SAUCE

This recipe is not suitable to freeze or microwave.

2 bacon rashers
2 beef eye fillet steaks
15g butter
1 tablespoon oil
1 medium onion, finely chopped
125g small mushrooms, sliced
3 teaspoons cornflour
1 cup water
¼ teaspoon mixed dried herbs
1 small beef stock cube, crumbled

1. Cut rind from bacon with scissors or sharp knife. Wrap 1 bacon rasher around each piece steak, secure bacon with metal skewer or toothpick.

2. Heat butter and oil in heavy-based frying pan, add steaks to pan. Cook over high heat for about 2 minutes or

until steaks are browned underneath. Turn steaks, cook over high heat until browned on other side. Reduce heat to medium, continue to cook steaks until they are cooked to suit individual tastes (see glossary). Remove steaks from pan to ovenproof dish, cover, place in slow oven to keep warm while making mushroom sauce.

3. Add onion to remaining butter mixture in pan, stir constantly over medium heat until onion is soft. Add mushrooms, stir constantly over

medium heat further 2 minutes or until mushrooms are just soft. Blend cornflour with a tablespoon of the water, stir in remaining water, herbs and stock cube, add to pan. Stir constantly over high heat until sauce boils and thickens. Place steaks on serving plates, pour sauce over, serve with vegetables of your choice, serve immediately.

Serves 2.

RIGHT: Filet Mignon with Mushroom Sauce.

China: Wedgwood; background: Abet Laminati

GRILLING

This popular method of cooking is suitable for the leaner, more expensive, tender cuts of beef that cook well in a short time. The same cut of beef can be used for pan-frying and for barbecuing.

Suitable cuts include T-bone steaks, porterhouse (T-bone without the bone), sirloin steaks cut from the hindquarter, rump steaks and fillet steaks. Less expensive cuts for grilling are the first 4 slices of round steak and the first 2 slices of topside steak. (If the beef is yearling, all the round steak is suitable for grilling and, though yearling topside is also suitable, it can be drier.)

Suitable cuts from the forequarter are rib steak on the bone, rib-eye steak, bolar blade steak, cross-cut or blade steak on the bone and oyster blade steak.

The time it takes to grill a piece of steak depends on the efficiency of the griller, the cut and thickness of the steak and, of course, how you like the steak cooked: rare, medium rare or well done (see glossary).

We have given you three delicious butters to serve with the steak. The butters can be used on other meat, fish and poultry, or eaten on bread like garlic butter.

Other foods suitable for grilling include lamb and pork, kidneys, sausages, chops, chicken, seafood and fruit.

GRILLED T-BONE STEAK WITH THREE BUTTERS

One quantity of each butter is sufficient for 8 large steaks (about 350g size). The butters can be refrigerated for up to a week ahead; keep wrapped in foil. They can be frozen for 3 months. Recipe unsuitable to microwave.

2 large T-bone steaks
PEPPERCORN BUTTER
250g butter, chopped
2 tablespoons canned drained green peppercorns
½ teaspoon ground black pepper
½ teaspoon dry mustard
MUSTARD BUTTER
250g butter, chopped
6 green shallots, chopped
2 tablespoons seeded mustard
1 tablespoon lemon juice
SATAY BUTTER
250g butter, chopped
4 small fresh red chillies, chopped
⅔ cup salted peanuts, chopped
1 tablespoon light soy sauce

1. Prepare butter of your choice by combining butter with remaining ingredients in small bowl of electric mixer or processor; beat or process until ingredients are just combined.

2. Spoon mixture onto piece of foil, press into triangle shape using 2 rulers or roll into sausage shape. Wrap foil firmly around butter, refrigerate for 30 minutes or until firm.

3. Trim as much fat as possible from steaks. Preheat griller on highest setting; this takes about 3 minutes. Curl tails around themselves, secure with toothpicks; place steaks on rack, grill for about 3 minutes or until steaks are changed in colour. Turn steaks, grill other side until changed in colour. Then grill until steaks are done to your liking. Turn steaks twice more during grilling to cook evenly. Serve immediately with butter of your choice.
    Serves 2.

ABOVE: Grilled T-Bone Steak.

China: Wedgwood

VEAL CHOPS

Veal chops are lean and are ideal for low-fat diets; they are particularly good in casseroles and stews. This tasty casserole is simple to make, and it can be served with rice or vegetables such as mashed potatoes (see glossary) and a green vegetable of your choice.

CASSEROLE OF VEAL AND TOMATOES

This casserole can be prepared up to 2 days ahead; keep, covered, in refrigerator. Casserole can be frozen for up to 2 months. See how to peel tomatoes in glossary. Recipe unsuitable to microwave.

2 large veal chops
¼ cup plain flour
1 tablespoon oil
1 medium onion, sliced
¼ cup dry white wine
1 small beef stock cube, crumbled
½ cup water
2 teaspoons sugar
2 medium tomatoes, peeled,
   chopped
1 teaspoon dried oregano leaves
6 black olives

1. Place chops in flour in bowl, press flour on lightly, shake off excess flour. Reserve 1 tablespoon of the flour. Heat oil in medium frying pan, add chops, cook over high heat until browned on both sides. Place chops in single layer in ovenproof dish. Add onion to pan, stir constantly over medium heat for about 3 minutes or until soft. Sprinkle the reserved flour over onion, stir constantly over medium heat until flour mixture is lightly browned.

BELOW: Casserole of Veal and Tomatoes.

Casserole dish: Inini

2. Gradually stir in combined wine, stock cube, water and sugar; stir constantly over high heat until mixture boils and thickens. Stir in tomatoes and oregano.

3. Pour into dish, cover with lid, bake in moderate oven for about 1 hour or until chops are tender. Add olives just before serving.
   Serves 2.

WIENER SCHNITZEL

Wiener schnitzel are traditionally pan-fried. We use a combination of oil and butter; the oil prevents the butter from burning during the cooking process. When pan-frying, veal needs to be protected by a coating of flour or crumbs to help stop it drying out. It is important not to over-cook veal or it will become tough and dry.

We like to use packaged and stale breadcrumbs in equal proportions; this gives a good-coloured but slightly soft coating on the veal (see glossary for how to prepare crumbs).

WIENER SCHNITZEL

Steaks can be crumbed a day ahead; keep, covered, in refrigerator. This recipe is unsuitable to freeze or microwave.

4 small veal steaks
¼ cup plain flour
1 egg, lightly beaten
¼ cup milk
½ cup packaged breadcrumbs
½ cup stale breadcrumbs
2 tablespoons oil
30g butter

1. Using sharp knife, cut membrane from around steaks; this will prevent steaks curling up during cooking.

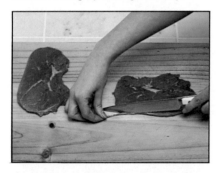

2. Use meat mallet to pound veal on both sides until it is fairly thin; trim steaks into neat shape.

3. Dust steaks lightly with flour, shake off excess flour.

4. Dip into combined egg and milk

5. Coat with combined breadcrumbs, press crumbs on firmly. Refrigerate 1 hour before cooking.

6. Heat oil and butter in large frying pan, add steaks, cook over medium heat for about 3 minutes on each side or until crumbs are golden brown; drain on absorbent paper. Serve immediately with hot vegetables or salad and lemon wedges to squeeze over schnitzels.

Serves 2.

RIGHT: Wiener Schnitzel.

TRIPE

Tripe is quite delicate in flavour, nutritious and easily digested; here we serve it with parsley sauce in a traditional, favourite recipe.

Tripe is the lining of the first and second stomachs of beef animals. There are several types. Honeycomb tripe is the best quality available. Tripe bought from the butcher has already been cleaned and partly cooked in a boiling process.

This dish is often served by itself. However, any vegetables of your choice can be used as an accompaniment. We served a julienne (see glossary) of partly cooked carrot and peppers.

TRIPE IN PARSLEY SAUCE

Tripe can be prepared up to a day ahead; keep, covered, in refrigerator. This recipe is unsuitable to freeze or microwave.

250g honeycomb tripe
2 teaspoons salt
1 small onion, sliced
2 whole cloves
1 bay leaf
2 cups milk
30g butter, softened
1 tablespoon plain flour
¼ cup chopped fresh parsley

1. Place tripe in large bowl, cover with cold water, add salt, stand for 1 hour. Drain tripe, cut into 1cm strips.

2. Combine tripe, onion, cloves, bay leaf and milk in medium saucepan, bring to boil, reduce heat, cover, simmer for about 45 minutes or until tripe is tender.

3. Combine butter and flour in small bowl, mix to a smooth paste with wooden spoon. Using slotted spoon, remove cloves and bay leaf from tripe mixture. Bring tripe mixture to the boil, add butter mixture; stir constantly over high heat until mixture boils and thickens, stir in parsley.

Serves 2.

TOP: Tripe in Parsley Sauce.

Plate: Lifestyle Imports

PORK

There is deluxe appeal about pork whether it is served as seasoned roast loin, as fillets, butterfly steaks or as that westernised Oriental favourite, sweet and sour pork. Generally, the flavour is heightened by sauces of many different types and flavours. In the past, pork was always cooked until it was well and truly over-done; there was a misconception that pork contained worms or some bacteria and these would affect health if they weren't destroyed by lengthy cooking. In fact, there has never been a problem of this kind in Australian pork, so cook pork as you would any other type of meat. Trim excess fat away first and cook meat only until it is tender but still moist. Over-cooking will destroy the texture and flavour.

PORK FILLETS

Pork and fruit are a delicious combination, and this dish is smart enough to serve at a dinner party. Pork fillets are boneless, lean pieces cut from the loin (ribs). They are fairly expensive but there is no waste. Be careful not to over-cook the pork as it will become dry; it should be just cooked so it retains its moist texture.

The sauce is a simple but colourful, tempting purée of the two fruits.

PORK FILLETS IN APRICOT MANGO SAUCE

Pork should be cooked just before serving for best results; sauce can be made a day ahead. Recipe unsuitable to freeze or microwave.

2 x 200g pork fillets
30g butter
APRICOT MANGO SAUCE
1 small mango, chopped
425g can unsweetened apricot halves

1. Using sharp knife, cut away any fat from pork.

2. Heat butter in frying pan, add pork; cook over high heat, turning often, until pork is lightly browned all over. Reduce heat, cook for further 10 minutes, uncovered, or until pork is tender; turn pork during cooking.

ABOVE: Pork Fillets in Apricot Mango Sauce.

3. Apricot Mango Sauce: Chop mango flesh; you need ¾ cup flesh for this recipe. Drain apricots, reserve ½ cup juice. Combine apricots, reserved juice and mango in blender or processor, blend until smooth. Heat sauce in small saucepan, without boiling, over low heat; serve with sliced pork and a green vegetable. Boiled rice (see glossary) would also be a good accompaniment.
Serves 2.

STIR-FRYING

Stir-frying food is a quick and easy method of cooking; the vegetables should be cooked only until they are beginning to tenderise. This method means that crispness, colour and good fresh flavour are retained.

The action of stir-frying is made easy by using a wok with a wok chan, like a little shovel (see picture). With it, the food is lifted and turned over quickly so it comes into contact frequently with the hot cooking surface of the wok.

We used a wok with top diameter of 33cm; it is a Chinese cooking pan shaped like a large bowl with a rounded base. This shape makes it ideal for cooking over gas burners. Flat-based woks are available for electric hot plates. The wide, open area of the wok facilitates quick, even cooking of food.

Woks are available in many sizes; the inexpensive variety available in stores which stock Asian food are ideal. Buy a wok chan which is designed to fit the inside of the wok at the same time.

To season a new wok before cooking, wash well with hot water and liquid detergent to remove any grease, wipe dry. Place wok over heat, add 2 tablespoons oil, 4 chopped green shallots and 1 clove crushed garlic. Swirl mixture over entire surface of wok, place over medium heat for 5 minutes. Discard mixture, rinse pan under warm water, wipe dry.

Do not scrub wok with any abrasive. Always wash in warm water, then wipe dry; this will protect the wok from rusting. Wipe over inside of wok with a lightly oiled cloth, cover with plastic wrap to prevent dust settling on the surface during storage.

Always heat wok before adding oil, then heat the oil before adding food to prevent food from sticking.

For this recipe, any meaty cuts of lean pork can be used; diced pork is available at most butchers and is ideal. The pork is best deep-fried in hot oil, see recipe for Salmon Patties for more details on deep-frying.

The vegetables in this recipe have been cut diagonally across the grain; see glossary for how to do this. Serve with rice (see glossary).

SWEET AND SOUR PORK

This recipe is not suitable to freeze or microwave.

750g pork loin chops
1 tablespoon cornflour
oil for deep frying
225g can unsweetened pineapple
 pieces
1 tablespoon cornflour, extra
1 tablespoon light soy sauce
1 tablespoon tomato sauce

1 tablespoon white vinegar
1 cup water
1 small cucumber
1 tablespoon oil, extra
1 medium onion, chopped
1 small red pepper, chopped
1 small green pepper, chopped
1 celery stick, chopped
1 medium carrot, chopped
2 green shallots, chopped

ABOVE: Sweet and Sour Pork.

Plate: Country Floors; wall panel: Pavillion Design

1. Trim fat and bones from chops; cut meat into 2cm cubes, toss in bowl with cornflour.

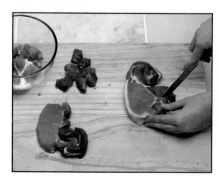

2. Heat oil, uncovered, over high heat in deep frying pan, add the pork in 2 batches, deep-fry for about 6 minutes or until pork is golden brown and tender; drain on absorbent paper.

3. Drain pineapple, reserve juice. Place extra cornflour in jug, stir in reserved juice, soy sauce, tomato sauce, vinegar and water. Cut cucumber in half lengthways, scoop out seeds with

teaspoon, chop cucumber into strips. Heat extra oil in wok over high heat, add onion, peppers and celery, stir-fry for about 3 minutes or until onion is soft. Add carrot, cucumber and pineapple pieces, stir-fry for 1 minute. **4.** Add pork and juice mixture, stir-fry over high heat until mixture boils and thickens. Serve immediately sprinkled with shallots.

Serves 4.

BUTTERFLY PORK STEAKS

Butterfly pork steaks are cuts from the middle loin area; these are split almost in half and opened out flat. Do not over-cook pork; this will make it tough and dry. We have given you a choice of 2 sauces: one savoury, flavoured with caraway; and the other, slightly sweet, flavoured with red currant jelly. Any cut of pork chops, steak or fillet can be used with these sauces.

BUTTERFLY PORK STEAKS WITH TWO SAUCES

Steaks are best prepared just before serving. This recipe is not suitable to freeze or microwave.

2 butterfly pork steaks
3 teaspoons oil
CARAWAY SAUCE
1 teaspoon caraway seeds
2 teaspoons plain flour
1 small chicken stock cube, crumbled
½ cup water
2 teaspoons tomato paste
1 tablespoon brown vinegar
1 teaspoon brown sugar
RED CURRANT JELLY SAUCE
2 teaspoons plain flour
1 small chicken stock cube, crumbled
½ cup water
1 tablespoon red currant jelly
1 tablespoon chopped fresh chives

1. Use sharp knife to trim excess fat from pork. Heat oil in large frying pan, add pork to pan in single layer. Cook over high heat for about 5 minutes on each side or until golden brown and tender. Remove pork from pan, cover, keep warm in very slow oven while making sauce. Drain away pan drippings except for 2 teaspoons.

2. Caraway Sauce: Heat pan drippings in frying pan, add seeds, cover, cook for about 1 minute or until seeds begin to crack. Add flour, stir constantly over high heat for about 1 minute or until mixture browns lightly.

3. Remove pan from heat, gradually stir in combined stock cube and water; stir until smooth. Stir in tomato paste, vinegar and sugar. Return pan to heat, stir constantly over high heat until mixture boils and thickens.

4. Red Currant Jelly Sauce: Heat pan drippings in frying pan, add flour, stir constantly over high heat until mixture browns lightly.

5. Remove pan from heat, gradually stir in the combined stock cube and water, stir until smooth. Return pan to heat, stir constantly over high heat until mixture boils and thickens.

6. Stir in jelly and chives, serve immediately. We like to leave small pieces of jelly suspended in the sauce; if you prefer, continue to stir over heat until jelly is melted. Serve with vegetables of your choice.

Serves 2.

RIGHT: Butterfly Pork Steaks with Red Currant Sauce (top) and Caraway Sauce (below).

China: Villeroy & Boch; rug: Australian East India Co.

ROAST LOIN OF PORK

The great thing about a loin of pork (or lamb) is that you can specify exactly how many chops you require in the one piece. Ask the butcher to cut you a loin of 4 chops; also ask him to score the rind, or you can cut a pretty pattern into the rind using a sharp knife. Make sure you cut down into the layer of fat under the rind.

You have the choice of asking for a boned-out loin where the bones are removed, or, if you want to retain the bones in the chops, the butcher will cut through the bones for you to simplify serving.

We chose a fruity seasoning for the pork which teams well with the traditional apple sauce.

TO PREPARE THE LOIN

1. Unroll loin and make a cut in the fleshy part, as shown; this gives you a place to put the seasoning.

2. Turn loin over, score rind with sharp knife. Make sure you cut down into the fat underneath the rind; this will help the rind to crisp and crackle during cooking time.

3. Place seasoning along flap, roll loin up firmly.

4. Tie loin together with strong string (synthetic string tends to slip).

ROAST PORK WITH APPLE SAUCE

Apple sauce can be prepared up to 2 days ahead; keep, covered, in refrigerator. Reheat, if preferred, just before serving. Recipe unsuitable to freeze or microwave.

1½kg boned loin of pork (equal to 4 chops)
1 tablespoon oil
2 teaspoons coarse cooking salt
200g kumara
2 large potatoes
1 tablespoon oil, extra
1 tablespoon grated parmesan cheese
100g broccoli
APRICOT SEASONING
⅓ cup stale breadcrumbs
¼ cup finely chopped dried apricots
2 tablespoons chopped walnuts or pecans
1 tablespoon chopped fresh parsley
3 teaspoons sweet sherry

Place pork in baking dish, bake in hot oven for about 20 minutes or until rind of pork begins to crackle. This can take a little less or more time.

Reduce oven temperature to moderate, bake further 1 hour or until the juices are clear when pork is pierced with skewer in meatiest part.

Add kumara and potatoes to the baking dish after the temperature has been reduced to moderate. Sprinkle potatoes with cheese; these will take 45 minutes to 1 hour to cook, depending on size of vegetables.

Do not turn pork or vegetables during cooking. An occasional (once or twice will do) basting or brushing with some of the pan drippings will be enough to brown the food.

To serve: Remove cooked pork from oven, cover with foil, stand 10 minutes to allow pork to become firm. Cut away string, slice pork thickly and place on heated serving plates (see Baked Dinner for hints on heating plates). Serve the kumara and potatoes and, last, the broccoli.

RIGHT: Roast Pork with Apple Sauce.

China: Royal Doulton; tiles: Northbridge Ceramic & Marble Centre

Apricot Seasoning: Combine bread-crumbs, apricots, nuts and parsley in medium bowl, stir in sherry; mix well.
Serves 2.

APPLE SAUCE

Apple Sauce is a traditional accompaniment to roast pork. You can buy canned pie apple and blend or process it until smooth, then sweeten it to your taste with sugar or honey. Or you can buy apple prepared for babies or bottled apple sauce ready to serve. However, it is quick and easy to make. We used a Granny Smith apple in this recipe. Recipe is not suitable to freeze.

1 small apple
1 tablespoon sugar
¼ cup water
pinch ground cinnamon
1. Peel apple, cut into quarters, remove core, slice apple.
2. Combine apple, sugar, water and cinnamon in medium saucepan. Cover, bring to boil, reduce heat, simmer, covered, for about 5 minutes or until apple is pulpy. Whisk or stir until apple mixture is smooth. Serve hot or cold.

MICROWAVE COOKING

Combine sliced apple with remaining ingredients in microwave-proof bowl, cover, cook on HIGH for about 3 minutes or until apple is soft. Whisk or stir as above.

TO PREPARE VEGETABLES

We chose to serve kumara, an orange-coloured sweet potato, roast potatoes and broccoli with the loin.
Broccoli: Boil, steam or microwave until tender; see glossary.
Kumara: This needs to be peeled with either a sharp knife or vegetable peeler and cut into pieces about the same size as half a large potato.
Potatoes: This method is slightly different from the potatoes served with Baked Dinner using lamb. Peel and halve the potatoes, place cut side down on a board and trim the ends away to give a neat shape. Using a sharp knife, cut the potato halves almost all the way through, as shown.
Place kumara and potatoes, cut side down, in a baking dish, brush all over with extra oil.

LAMB

A baked dinner of lamb with crispy brown potatoes, pumpkin, mint sauce and gravy is a treat for many of us, as are other lamb dishes enjoyed since childhood. A baked dinner is equally welcome as a family-style dinner or for a special occasion, so are crusty racks of lamb. Then there are crunchy crumbed cutlets and a quick and easy curry you will enjoy trying. All can be mastered quickly. Remember, lamb is nicer and healthier to eat if you trim away as much fat as possible before cooking. There is a modern trend towards serving lamb which is under-cooked so the meat is pink and juicy, as for beef; this is a matter of personal taste and acceptance. However, avoid over-cooking lamb as it tends to be dry, grey and loses much of its flavour.

RACKS OF LAMB

Racks of lamb are simply cutlets joined together. They can be cooked flat or standing, as in our picture; this makes them look special for a dinner party.

You can ask the butcher to cut a rack of 2 or as many cutlets as you require. A rack of 6 is a manageable number. Allow 2 or 3 cutlets per person, depending on the size of the cutlets. Cover exposed cutlet bones with pieces of foil during cooking so they won't over-cook.

The delicious crust makes the racks more attractive and adds flavour. The crust tends to fall off if you cut the racks too soon after cooking, so allow them to stand for about 5 minutes before cutting. Racks are easy to serve; use a sharp knife to cut between each cutlet.

RACKS OF LAMB WITH SWEET GARLIC AND HERB CRUST

Lamb can be prepared with the crust up to a day ahead; keep, covered, in refrigerator. Finely chopped fresh mint or basil can be substituted for fresh rosemary, if preferred. Recipe unsuitable to freeze or microwave.

2 racks of lamb (6 cutlets in each)
2 cloves garlic, crushed
2 tablespoons chopped fresh parsley
2 teaspoons chopped fresh rosemary
2 teaspoons chopped fresh chives
2 teaspoons brown sugar
½ cup stale breadcrumbs
1 small chicken stock cube, crumbled
1 tablespoon lemon juice
30g butter, melted

1. Using sharp knife, trim away excess fat from outside of racks.

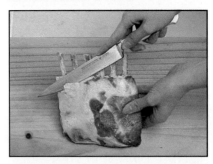

2. Place racks upright in baking dish, cover each bone with foil.

3. Combine remaining ingredients in medium bowl, stir until well mixed.

4. Press crumb mixture firmly onto each rack of lamb. Bake in moderate oven for about 45 minutes or until cooked as desired. Stand racks for 5 minutes to make cutting easier. Serve with vegetables of your choice. (For baked vegetables, see Baked Dinner and Roast Loin of Pork.)
Serves 4.

LEFT: Racks of Lamb with Sweet Garlic and Herb Crust.

Platter & carvers: Chelsea House Antiques; table: The Royal Trading Company; tea-towel: Appley Hoare Antiques

BAKED DINNER

A leg of lamb which has had the bone removed is called a butterflied leg. This method makes it easy to cut away as much fat as you like before cooking and shortens cooking time. The cooking is more even and, best of all, the meat slices easily into neat pieces.

You can bone the leg of lamb yourself, using our picture as a guide or you can ask the butcher to do this for you.

HEATING DINNER PLATES

The hardest part of baking a dinner is to keep it hot while you are serving it onto the plates. It helps if the plates are hot. You can heat plates in several different ways.

Place them in a slow oven for about 15 minutes. Or if your stove has a griller above the oven, it will probably be hot enough from the heat from the oven to warm the plates there; simply place them in the grill compartment for about 20 to 30 minutes.

Plates can be heated in a microwave oven by placing pieces of damp absorbent paper between the plates (remember, silver or gold-trimmed plates can't be used in a microwave oven as the metal content causes "arcing" and possible damage to the oven).

Plates can also be heated by standing them in a sink of very hot water for a few minutes; dry thoroughly before using.

Some ovens have warming ovens or drawers for warming plates; check the manufacturer's instructions.

SERVING A HOT DINNER

The main thing is to have everything ready for serving.

The baked vegetables will keep hottest longest, so put them on the plates first, then the meat, the sauce and finally the peas.

If your oven size permits, the plates with the food on can be returned to the oven on moderate for about 10 minutes but take care if you do this, as over-heating will make the food look dry and unappetising.

The microwave oven is superb for reheating whole meals. Simply cover the plates with a microwave-safe polyethylene plastic food wrap and microwave on HIGH for at least 30 seconds, depending on how hot the food was before microwaving.

RIGHT: Baked Lamb Dinner with Vegetables.

BAKED LAMB DINNER WITH VEGETABLES

Mint sauce is served cold as an accompaniment to lamb and can be prepared up to a week ahead; keep, covered, in refrigerator. Recipe unsuitable to freeze or microwave.

1½kg leg of lamb
¼ teaspoon ground black pepper
½ teaspoon paprika
2 teaspoons fresh rosemary leaves
1 clove garlic, crushed
2 tablespoons oil
4 medium potatoes
400g pumpkin
4 medium onions
1 tablespoon oil, extra
1 cup fresh or frozen peas
GRAVY
1½ tablespoons plain flour
1 teaspoon chopped fresh rosemary
    leaves
1½ cups water
½ small beef stock cube, crumbled
1 teaspoon Worcestershire sauce
MINT SAUCE
1 tablespoon sugar
2 tablespoons water
⅓ cup brown vinegar
¼ cup chopped fresh mint

1. To butterfly lamb: Using sharp knife, cut down the length of the bone as shown, then cut meat from around both bones. Cut away as much fat as possible.

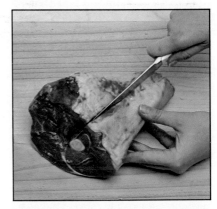

2. Combine pepper, paprika, rosemary, garlic and oil in small bowl, mix well. Using hand, rub oil mixture all over both sides of lamb.

41

3. Place lamb fat side up on rack over baking dish. Brush or rub potatoes, pumpkin and onions with a little extra oil, place on rack next to lamb, if space permits. If it doesn't, place in shallow pan (such as lamington pan) or on oven tray. Deep-sided pans will prevent vegetables from browning.

Bake in moderate oven for about 45 minutes or until lamb is tender and juices are clear when lamb is pierced with a skewer in the thickest part.

Remove lamb from oven, leave vegetables in oven to continue to crisp while you are cooking the peas. Cover lamb tightly with foil while making gravy; this standing time allows the lamb time to become firm enough to slice. It will stay hot enough for about 10 minutes.

Gravy: Pour pan drippings from baking dish except for 2 tablespoons. Place baking dish over heat, add flour, stir constantly over high heat until flour is lightly browned; scrape as much of the coloured bits and pieces from the base of the dish as you can. These will flavour and colour the gravy. Remove dish from heat.

Gradually stir in combined rosemary, water, stock cube and Worcestershire sauce. Return to high heat, stir constantly until mixture boils and thickens; strain into small saucepan (cover to prevent skin forming). Reheat when necessary.

Cut lamb into enough neat slices for your diners, pour any juices from the lamb back into the saucepan of gravy. Cover lamb tightly with foil, return to oven to keep warm.

Mint Sauce: Combine sugar and water in small saucepan, stir constantly over high heat, without boiling, until sugar is dissolved; bring to boil, boil 2 minutes, without stirring. Remove from heat, add vinegar and mint. Reheat before serving, if you prefer.

Serves 4.

TO PREPARE VEGETABLES

Potatoes: Cut peeled potatoes in half, steam for 5 minutes or drop into saucepan with enough boiling water to just cover potatoes, boil for 5 minutes. Drain potatoes, use tongs to transfer potatoes to absorbent paper to drain and until they are cool enough to handle. Use fork to score upper rounded surface and make it rough; this will help potatoes to become crisp during baking.

Pumpkin: Any type of pumpkin can be baked; these include the larger type or the smaller, sweeter varieties such as butternut or golden nugget. Cut

pumpkin into chunks a little larger than the pieces of potato. Pumpkin doesn't take quite as long to cook as potatoes.

Leave skin on, if you like (it is edible) or cut skin away with sharp knife. The skin is easy to cut from pumpkin which has been microwaved on HIGH for a minute or 2; the time taken depends on the type and size of the pieces of pumpkin.

Onions: Brown onions are the best for baking; try to choose onions of even size. Peel away 1 or 2 layers of skin, leaving a little of the root end intact to hold onions together during baking.

TO COOK PEAS

Boil or microwave peas so they are cooked at the same time as the baked vegetables are ready to serve.

Frozen peas should be added to medium saucepan half-full of boiling water; allow peas to return to boil, uncovered; reduce heat, simmer for about 3 minutes (or microwave in microwave-proof dish for about 5 minutes) or until tender.

Fresh peas should be boiled or microwaved for about twice as long as frozen peas.

If using dehydrated peas, allow 7 minutes cooking time after they reach boiling point; check the instructions on the packet.

LAMB'S FRY

Lamb's fry is lamb's liver, always a great favourite for breakfast; serve it with crisp grilled or pan-fried bacon and hot toast. It would also make a good snack or brunch dish.

LAMB'S FRY WITH BACON

This recipe is not suitable to freeze or microwave.

1 lamb's fry
2 teaspoons salt
¼ cup plain flour
15g butter
2 tablespoons oil
1¼ cups water
1 small beef stock cube, crumbled
2 tablespoons tomato sauce
2 teaspoons Worcestershire sauce
2 tablespoons chopped fresh parsley

1. Place lamb's fry in bowl, cover with cold water, add salt, stand for 1 hour; drain. Carefully peel membrane from fry, using sharp knife.

2. Using sharp knife, cut fry crosswise into thin slices, as shown. Combine fry and flour in plastic bag, shake well to coat fry with flour.

3. Heat butter and oil in frying pan, add fry; reserve excess flour in bag. Cook fry for about 2 minutes on each side; do not over-cook as fry will be tough and dry. Remove from pan, drain on absorbent paper.

ABOVE: Lamb's Fry and Bacon.

Plate: Dansab

4. Add reserved flour to pan, stir constantly over high heat for about 1 minute or until mixture is lightly browned. Remove from heat, gradually add combined water and stock cube, sauces and parsley, return to heat, stir constantly over high heat until mixture boils and thickens. Return cooked fry to sauce, heat gently without boiling; stir occasionally to coat fry well with sauce. Serve immediately.

Serves 2.

LAMBS' BRAINS

Brains are sold in sets of 2 (or pairs); they make an ideal dish for breakfast, lunch or a snack. Short cooking time is all that's required for this delicately-flavoured food. Long cooking will simply dry and toughen the brains.

It is important to remove the membrane completely from the brains or it will become tough during the cooking time.

CRUMBED FRIED BRAINS

Brains can be crumbed several hours ahead; keep, covered, in refrigerator. This recipe is not suitable to freeze or microwave.

2 sets lambs' brains
2 tablespoons plain flour
1 egg, lightly beaten

⅓ cup packaged dry breadcrumbs, approximately
oil for deep frying

1. Place brains in bowl, cover with cold water, stand 1 hour, drain. Cut each set of brains in half, as shown; remove detached parts from underneath. Carefully peel away membrane; using a toothpick makes the task easier.

2. Place brains into medium saucepan with enough cold water to barely cover the brains, bring to boil, reduce heat, simmer, uncovered, for 2 minutes. Remove brains from water, drain on absorbent paper. Toss brains lightly in flour in a plastic bag, dip into egg, then coat firmly with breadcrumbs.

3. Heat oil in deep medium saucepan (see Salmon Patties for further information on deep-frying). Deep-fry brains in hot oil for a few minutes or until golden brown, drain on absorbent paper. Serve immediately with a squeeze of lemon juice, if desired.
Serves 2.

LEFT: Crumbed Fried Brains.

Plate & fork: Dansab

LAMBS' KIDNEYS

Lambs' kidneys have a distinct flavour; buy them as close to cooking time as possible. They are often served for breakfast or as a light meal. You can serve rice (see glossary) or potatoes with them if you prefer to serve them as a heartier meal.

GRILLED KIDNEYS WITH RED CURRANT SAUCE

Bamboo skewers need to be soaked in water before use (see Chicken Satay recipe for more details about skewers). Sauce can be prepared up to a day ahead; keep, covered, in refrigerator. Recipe unsuitable to freeze or microwave.

6 lambs' kidneys
ground black pepper
15g butter
1 medium onion, sliced
RED CURRANT SAUCE
2 tablespoons red currant jelly
2 teaspoons French mustard
1½ teaspoons plain flour
⅓ cup water
1½ teaspoons lemon juice
**½ small chicken stock cube,
   crumbled**
1 tablespoon port

1. Place kidneys in medium bowl, add enough cold water to cover, stand for 1 hour. Peel away membrane. Cut kidneys in half lengthwise, drain on absorbent paper. Remove hard core and any fat from centres of kidney halves. Pre-heat griller to high.

2. Thread 3 kidney halves onto each skewer, sprinkle kidneys with a little pepper, place under pre-heated griller, cut sides up. Grill kidneys for about 3 minutes on each side or until tender; do not over-cook or kidneys will be tough and dry. Remove kidneys from skewers to serving plates.

While kidneys are cooking, melt butter in frying pan, add onion, cook, stirring occasionally, over medium heat for about 5 minutes, or until onion is soft and lightly browned. Serve over kidneys, top with red currant sauce.

3. Red Currant Sauce: While kidneys are grilling and onions are frying, prepare sauce. Place jelly in small saucepan, stir constantly over low heat until jelly is melted, stir in mustard. Blend flour with water in small bowl, stir in lemon juice and stock cube, stir into jelly. Stir constantly over medium heat until mixture boils and thickens; stir in port.
   Serves 2.

RIGHT: Grilled Kidneys with Red Currant Sauce.

Tiles: Pazotti

QUICK CURRIED LAMB

This is a slightly sweet Australian family style of curry. It is made easy and quick by using prepared curry powder instead of mixing your own spices in the traditional method.

Only trial and error will help you find the curry powder with the flavour you like best, and the amount to use of that powder. Buy small quantities at a time and keep in an airtight container away from the light.

We used chump chops in this recipe; they take a short time to cook. Other cuts suitable for curries are cuts from the leg, shoulder, forequarter and neck. Simply cook the curry until the lamb is tender; neck chops will take the longest cooking time.

We served our curry with boiled rice (see glossary), and added a tiny pinch of saffron powder to the water while it was boiling to give the rice the yellow colour you see in the picture.

Pappadams are a traditional accompaniment to curry; they can be bought in several sizes and many flavours, are quick and easy to cook and add a crunchy texture to the meal. Check instructions on the packet for cooking methods or cook them in a microwave oven in a single layer on a plate or turntable on HIGH for about 1 minute for 4 small pappadams.

EASY LAMB AND TOMATO CURRY

We used a Granny Smith apple in this recipe. To peel tomato, see glossary. Curry can be prepared up to 2 days ahead; keep, covered, in refrigerator. Curry will freeze for 2 months. Recipe unsuitable to microwave.

4 lamb chump chops
1 tablespoon oil
1 clove garlic, finely chopped
1 small onion, finely sliced
1 tablespoon curry powder
1 medium tomato, peeled, chopped
¼ cup water
1 small apple, chopped
1 tablespoon sultanas

1. Using sharp knife, cut away the excess fat and bones from chops. Cut meat into 3cm pieces.

2. Heat oil in medium saucepan, add garlic, onion and curry powder, then stir constantly over heat for about 3 minutes or until onion is soft. Stir in tomato and water, stir constantly over heat for 1 minute.

3. Add meat to pan, stir constantly over high heat until meat is well coated with curry mixture.

4. Bring to boil, reduce heat, simmer, covered, for about 30 minutes or until lamb is tender. Stir in apple and sultanas; simmer, covered, further 5 minutes or until apple is tender.

Serves 2.

RIGHT: Easy Lamb and Tomato Curry.

Bowl: Corso de Fiori

LAMB CUTLETS

Lamb cutlets have always been a great favourite. Allow 2 or 3 cutlets for each person, depending on the size of the cutlets. Crumbed cutlets are usually shallow-fried in oil or oil and butter until they are golden brown and cooked through. We prefer the healthier alternative of oven-baking where you need only a little oil.

Marinating or standing the cutlets in the soy sauce and garlic mixture imparts a delicious flavour to the cutlets. The salt-reduced soy sauce has a delicate flavour which teams well with lamb.

Stale or packaged breadcrumbs can be used, but we prefer a combination of both.

Mashed potatoes (see glossary) and a green vegetable such as peas, beans or broccoli are usually served with crumbed cutlets.

CRUMBED MARINATED LAMB CUTLETS

Cutlets can be crumbed up to a day ahead; keep, covered, in refrigerator. This recipe is not suitable to freeze or microwave.

6 small lamb cutlets
2 tablespoons salt-reduced
  soy sauce
1 clove garlic, crushed
¼ cup plain flour
1 egg, lightly beaten
1 tablespoon milk
½ cup stale breadcrumbs,
  approximately
½ cup packaged dry breadcrumbs,
  approximately
1 tablespoon oil

1. Trim excess fat from cutlets. Using meat mallet, pound each cutlet between sheets of plastic wrap until cutlets are slightly flattened.

2. Combine soy sauce and garlic in dish, mix well. Add cutlets, cover, marinate 30 minutes; turn several times during marinating.

3. Place flour into plastic bag, add cutlets, toss until cutlets are well coated with flour.

4. Dip cutlets into combined egg and milk, then coat with combined breadcrumbs. Brush a shallow oven tray with oil, place cutlets onto tray in single layer.

5. Bake cutlets in moderate oven for 15 minutes; turn cutlets over, bake further 15 minutes or until cutlets are golden brown and tender.

Serves 2.

RIGHT: Crumbed Marinated Lamb Cutlets.

Plate: Country Floors

CHICKEN

Chicken is incredibly versatile and seems to have an all-round acceptance. We have included quite a variety of cooking methods for different chicken cuts. They include roasting, pan-frying, casseroling, poaching and oven-baking. We used the young, tender roasting chickens for all our recipes; boiling fowls are older and tougher and require pressure cooking, pot roasting, boiling or braising to tenderise them. The numbering system applied to chickens is easy to follow; No. 15 means the chicken is 1.5kg; No. 13 means the chicken is 1.3kg and so on. Chickens can be bought fresh or frozen; follow thawing instructions on the bag. Chickens should not be cooked until they are thawed completely. Some chickens have small plastic bags containing the neck and/or giblets; remove these before cooking.

CHICKEN 'N' CHIPS

Chicken 'n' chips has become a great favourite since chickens have become so inexpensive and plentiful. As a guide, a No. 15 chicken will serve 2 adults and 2 children, provided there are vegetables or salad to make the meal adequate. We chose lettuce, tomato and cucumber with a French dressing (see Rice Salad for how to make the dressing).

The roast chicken can be served as a complete baked dinner with vegetables, if you prefer (see Roast Loin of Pork and Baked Dinner for suggested vegetable accompaniments to this meal).

SEASONED ROAST CHICKEN

Use good strong string for trussing chicken; synthetic string tends to slip and some types will not withstand the heat of the oven.

Seasoning can be prepared up to a day ahead. Seasoned chicken can be frozen for 2 months.

This recipe can be cooked in the microwave oven but it will not look the same as ours, which was roasted in the conventional way.

Follow your oven manufacturer's directions for good results.

Chips cannot be deep-fried in the microwave oven.

No. 15 chicken
15g butter, melted
SEASONING
1½ cups stale breadcrumbs
1 stick celery, finely chopped
1 small onion, finely chopped
1 teaspoon dried mixed herbs
1 egg, lightly beaten
CHIPS
4 large potatoes
oil for deep frying

1. Remove and discard any fat from cavity of chicken.

2. Fill cavity of chicken with seasoning mixture; do not pack seasoning in tightly because bread expands during cooking and the seasoning will become a solid mass.

3. Place chicken on board, breast-side-up. Secure chicken with string by looping string around tail end; bring string around ends of drumsticks (legs). Following the creases between the drumsticks and body, take string towards wing end of chicken.

4. Turn chicken breast-side-down and secure string around wings, as shown.

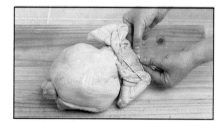

5. Place chicken on rack over baking dish. Half-fill baking dish with water; it should not touch the chicken. Brush chicken with butter, a small pastry brush is good for this; bake in moderately hot oven for 15 minutes; reduce heat to moderate, bake further 1½ hours. Pierce skin and flesh of chicken in the thickest part of the

ABOVE: Seasoned Roast Chicken with Chips.

Platter and covered gravy boat: Noritake

drumstick; the juices will be clear if the chicken is cooked. Or, wriggle the leg of the chicken and it will feel quite loose at the joint; this indicates the chicken is cooked. Stand chicken 10 minutes before breaking or cutting into serving-sized pieces. Poultry shears or strong scissors do a good job of cutting chicken.

6. Seasoning: Combine breadcrumbs, celery, onion, herbs and egg in medium bowl with hand or wooden spoon; mix well.

REALLY GOOD CHIPS

The secret of making good chips, which are crisp on the outside and soft and fluffy on the inside, depends largely on the type of potato used. Experiment until you find the type that suits your taste best. Generally, a hard, dry potato such as Pontiac or Kennebec will give good results.

If making a large quantity of chips, invest in a deep-sided, wide-topped frying pan with a frying basket to suit the size of the pan. The double frying method of cooking chips will give you the best results. After the first fry, the temperature of the oil will drop. Reheat the oil then fry the chips until done.

1. Peel potatoes, cut into 1cm slices then into 1cm strips, or finer, if you prefer. Dry chips thoroughly with tea-towel before frying.

2. Heat enough oil in deep frying pan to come halfway up side of pan (see Salmon Patties for more details on deep-frying). Add chips gradually so oil won't spatter. Cook for a few minutes or until they barely change colour; drain well on absorbent paper.

3. Fry chips again until light golden brown. Drain well on absorbent paper, serve immediately.

CUTTING UP A CHICKEN

This recipe for a tasty casserole is to show you how to cut up a whole chicken into large, serving-sized pieces. Of course, you can buy chicken pieces or buy all of the same kind of chicken cut. You will need 1½kg chicken pieces for 4 serves.

CHICKEN AND FRENCH ONION CASSEROLE

Casserole can be prepared up to the stage just before cooking a day ahead. If you omit sour cream and parsley, casserole can be cooked and frozen for up to 2 months; however, the sauce might become watery during reheating. If this happens, blend another 2 tablespoons plain flour or 1 tablespoon cornflour with an equal amount of water and stir into the dish when it reaches boiling point. Return to boil while stirring constantly; stir in sour cream and parsley.

This recipe can be cooked in a microwave-proof dish, covered, in the microwave oven after the chicken, onion and bacon have been fried as directed. Cooking time will be about 20 minutes. Casserole will taste more salty cooked in this way.

No. 15 chicken
2 tablespoons plain flour
30g packet French onion soup mix
30g butter
2 tablespoons oil
3 bacon rashers, chopped
2 medium onions, sliced
1 cup water
2 tablespoons sour cream
2 tablespoons chopped fresh parsley
1. Cut through skin connecting legs to body, then find with your fingers the joints between legs and body and cut through these; the cuts which consist of the combined legs and thighs are called marylands.

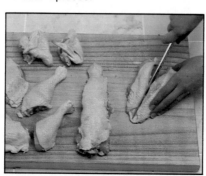

2. Cut maryland pieces into 2 at joint to give thigh and leg (drumstick).

3. Cut a small amount of breast meat with the wing, then bend wing away from body to find joint where wing joins body; cut through this.

4. Separate breast and back by cutting through rib bones along each side of body; cut close to the backbone.

5. Cut along breast bone to divide breast into 2 pieces. Trim away excess fat and skin from all pieces. The back portion can be cut into 2 and added to the casserole; it is not very meaty and is best used for soup or stock. Freeze the back portion until you accumulate at least 4 pieces.

6. Combine chicken pieces with flour and dry soup mix in plastic bag, toss well to coat chicken with mixture (reserve excess flour mixture). Heat butter and oil in flameproof dish, add chicken in single layer. Cook chicken, turning often, until browned all over.

ABOVE: Chicken and French Onion Casserole.

Casserole dish: Opus

7. Remove chicken from dish, add bacon and onions; stir constantly over heat for about 3 minutes or until onions are soft.

8. Return chicken to dish with blended reserved flour mixture and water (see glossary), cover, bake in moderate oven for about 1 hour or until chicken is tender.

9. Stir in sour cream and parsley just before serving. Serve with rice or pasta (see glossary).
Serves 4.

POACHED CHICKEN

Cold poached chicken dressed up with a herb mayonnaise makes a light meal ideal for lunch, when served with a salad. It could also be served as an attractive entrée for 6 people; serve only 2 or 3 small slices of the chicken, with salad vegetables as a garnish.

Chicken breast fillets are available in chicken shops, some delicatessens and butchers. They are usually sold skinless and boneless. Remove fat before cooking.

The stock in which the chicken is cooked can be reserved then boiled rapidly in an uncovered saucepan until it is reduced to a bit less than half the original quantity.

Cool this more concentrated stock and freeze it for future use as stock instead of water and stock cubes in recipes, or as a base for soup.

Chicken can be poached, covered, in a microwave-proof dish on HIGH for about 2½ minutes. Use hot water; by the time the water comes to the boil the chicken should be cooked. It is easy to over-cook chicken in the microwave oven, so check constantly during cooking time.

CHICKEN BREASTS WITH BASIL MAYONNAISE

Basil mayonnaise can be made several hours ahead; keep surface of mayonnaise covered with plastic wrap or greaseproof paper. Chicken can be poached a day before required; keep, covered, in refrigerator. Recipe unsuitable to freeze.

2 cups water
¼ cup dry white wine
1 small chicken stock cube, crumbled
1 bay leaf
2 chicken breast fillets
BASIL MAYONNAISE
¼ cup mayonnaise
2 teaspoons chopped fresh basil
1 small clove garlic, crushed
2 teaspoons grated parmesan cheese
1 teaspoon water

1. Combine water, wine, stock cube and bay leaf in shallow frying pan; add

chicken. If necessary, add extra water to barely cover chicken. Bring to boil, reduce heat, simmer, uncovered, for about 10 minutes or until chicken is tender. Do not over-cook or chicken will be dry and tough. Remove chicken from stock, cool chicken to room temperature, cover, refrigerate.

2. Basil Mayonnaise: Combine mayonnaise, basil, garlic, cheese and water in medium bowl; mix well.

3. Using sharp knife, cut chicken on an angle into neat slices. Place chicken on serving plates, top with basil mayonnaise, serve with salad vegetables of your choice.

Serves 2.

RIGHT: Chicken Breasts with Basil Mayonnaise.

Plate: Lifestyle Imports

CHICKEN BREAST FILLETS

Skinless, boneless breast fillets are popular for guests and family alike, and this simple green peppercorn sauce makes them extra special.

PAN-FRIED CHICKEN WITH GREEN PEPPERCORN SAUCE

Canned green peppercorns are imported and are available from gourmet sections of supermarkets and delicatessens. This dish is at its best prepared just before serving. Recipe unsuitable to freeze or microwave.

2 chicken breast fillets
30g butter
1 tablespoon plain flour
1 small chicken stock cube, crumbled
½ cup water
2 teaspoons drained canned green peppercorns
1 tablespoon cream

1. Trim any excess fat from chicken. Melt butter in small frying pan, add

chicken, cook over medium heat for about 10 minutes or until tender and lightly browned; turn several times during cooking. Remove chicken from pan, cover with foil to keep warm.
2. Sprinkle flour into frying pan, stir constantly over high heat until mixture is lightly browned.

3. Remove from heat, gradually stir in combined stock cube and water, return to heat, stir constantly over high heat until sauce boils and thickens.

4. Add peppercorns and cream to sauce, stir over high heat, without boiling, until sauce is heated through. Serve immediately over chicken.
Serves 2.

TOP: Pan-Fried Chicken with Green Peppercorn Sauce.

Plate: Noritake

CHICKEN WINGS

Wings are tasty; some say they are the sweetest, most tender parts of the bird. They are inexpensive and are perfect finger food for parties, or serve them as a meal; children love them!

Oven-baking makes these wings easy to handle and a lot can be cooked at the one time. They can also be grilled or barbecued slowly; however, watch them carefully as the honey tends to burn.

OVEN-BAKED HONEYED CHICKEN WINGS

Uncooked wings and marinade can be kept, covered, in the refrigerator for 2 days, or frozen for up to 2 months. Recipe unsuitable to microwave.

500g chicken wings
1 tablespoon light soy sauce
1 tablespoon dark soy sauce
1 tablespoon lemon juice
1 tablespoon dry sherry
1 tablespoon sesame seeds
1 teaspoon grated fresh ginger
2 tablespoons honey
¼ teaspoon sesame oil

1. Tuck wing tips under main part of wings, place wings into large bowl.

2. Combine sauces, juice, sherry, seeds, ginger, honey and oil in jug, pour over wings. Cover, refrigerate for at least 1 hour; overnight is better. All wings should be coated with marinade.

3. Place wings on rack o[...] dish, bake in moderate oven [...] 30 minutes or until tender. Du[...] time, brush with remaining m[...] and turn every 10 minutes.

Serves 2.

BELOW: Oven-Baked Honeyed Chicken Wings.

Plate: Australian East India Co.

CHICKEN DRUMSTICKS

These oven-baked chicken drumsticks (legs) make good snack or finger food; they can also be served as a main meal with vegetables or salad.

The amount of curry powder specified in this recipe will not give a lot of heat to the coating; you can increase it if you prefer.

CHICKEN AND YOGHURT DRUMSTICKS

Chicken can be marinated in yoghurt up to a day ahead; keep, covered, in refrigerator. Recipe unsuitable to freeze or microwave.

6 medium chicken drumsticks
1 clove garlic, finely chopped
3 teaspoons curry powder
½ cup plain yoghurt
½ teaspoon ground cumin
50g packet potato crisps

1. Using sharp knife, cut slits in drumsticks about 1cm apart.

2. Combine garlic, curry powder, yoghurt and cumin in medium bowl, stir until smooth. Add drumsticks, mix until drumsticks are well coated with yoghurt mixture Place crisps in plastic bag, crush with rolling pin until fairly fine, place in lamington pan.

3. Coat drumsticks with crisps, place on greased oven tray in single layer. Bake in moderate oven for about 30 minutes or until drumsticks are tender.

Makes 6.

BELOW: Chicken and Yoghurt Drumsticks.

Plate: Cass Shopping; background: Abet Laminati

CHICKEN SATAY

Satays are tasty little morsels to serve as a snack, at a barbecue or as a meal on a bed of rice (see glossary).

Chicken breast or thigh fillets can be used for this recipe but we prefer the flavour of thigh fillets.

Use either stainless steel or wooden skewers for satays. Stainless steel skewers are unsuitable for use in the microwave oven but are ideal for barbecuing, grilling and frying. The advantage of these skewers is that you can use, wash and use them again.

Wooden skewers need to be soaked in water to help minimise burning during cooking. They need at least an hour. However, if you're organised enough, overnight is best.

Wooden skewers are disposed of after use because at least 1 end is burnt during cooking. Keep exposed wood away from flame or elements.

Satays can be cooked on a flat, microwave-proof dish in the microwave oven but will not be browned and have more of a steamed flavour. They can also be cooked on a brown-ing dish; follow the oven manufacturer's instructions.

TOP: Chicken Satay with Peanut Sauce.

Plate: Made in Japan

CHICKEN SATAY WITH PEANUT SAUCE

Skewers with chicken can be prepared a day ahead; keep, covered, in refrigerator, or freeze for 2 months.

500g chicken thigh fillets
1 tablespoon oil
30g butter
PEANUT SAUCE
½ cup crunchy peanut butter
¼ cup plain yoghurt
1 tablespoon sweet fruit chutney
1 tablespoon lemon juice
2 teaspoons light soy sauce
1 tablespoon dry sherry
1 small fresh red chilli, finely chopped
3 green shallots, chopped
¼ teaspoon ground cumin
½ teaspoon curry powder
1 teaspoon grated fresh ginger
1. Cut away excess fat from fillets, cut fillets lengthwise into strips about 1½cm wide.

2. Thread strips of chicken onto soaked skewers; we used 10 skewers.

3. Heat oil and butter in medium frying pan. Add satay sticks to pan in single layer and cook over heat for about 4 minutes; turn satay sticks frequently during cooking. Serve immediately with sauce.

Peanut Sauce: Combine peanut butter, yoghurt, chutney, lemon juice, soy sauce, sherry, chilli, shallots, cumin, curry powder and ginger in medium bowl, mix well.

Makes 10.

STIR-FRIED CHICKEN

This is a good way to extend chicken into a hearty, nourishing, vitamin-packed meal. Serve with rice (see glossary). If you don't like the flavour of garlic or ginger, leave them out. You can also omit the chilli, if preferred. The flavour of the dish will still be excellent.

CHILLI CHICKEN AND VEGETABLE STIR-FRY

We have cooked this dish in a wok, using a wok chan for stir-frying; see Sweet and Sour Pork recipe for details on wok cookery. Dish is best made just before serving. Recipe unsuitable to freeze or microwave.

250g chicken thigh fillets
1 medium carrot
1 stick celery
1 small red pepper
1 tablespoon oil
1 clove garlic, finely chopped
1 small fresh red chilli, finely chopped
½ teaspoon grated fresh ginger
1 small onion, finely sliced
2 teaspoons light soy sauce
1 tablespoon oyster sauce
1 teaspoon sesame oil
1 teaspoon sugar

1. Remove any fat from chicken. Cut chicken into thin strips, as shown.

2. Cut carrot, celery and pepper into thin strips, as shown.

3. Heat oil in wok or large frying pan. Add garlic, chilli, ginger and onion, stir-fry over high heat for about 2 minutes or until onion is soft. Stir in chicken and carrot, stir-fry over high heat until chicken is tender.

4. Add celery and pepper, stir-fry for about 2 minutes or until celery is just tender. Stir in combined sauces, sesame oil and sugar.
Serves 2.

TOP: Chilli Chicken and Vegetable Stir-Fry.

Plate: Made in Japan; tiles: Northbridge Ceramic & Marble Centre

CHICKEN THIGH FILLETS

The cooking method of pan-frying is ideal for chicken thigh fillets. They are small, tasty, boneless and skinless pieces cut from the thigh; they have a texture different from breast fillets. Allow at least 2 fillets for each person.

PAN-FRIED CHICKEN WITH TOMATO BACON SAUCE

Sauce can be made up to a day ahead; keep, covered, in refrigerator. Dish can be frozen for up to 2 months. The sauce can be made in a microwave-proof dish. To do this, cook bacon and onion first on HIGH for about 3 minutes or until onion is soft. Add remaining ingredients, cook on HIGH for about 5 minutes or until thick.

2 bacon rashers, chopped
1 medium onion, finely chopped
1 clove garlic, crushed
410g can tomatoes
¼ cup water
1 tablespoon tomato paste
¼ teaspoon dried basil leaves
¼ teaspoon dried oregano leaves
¼ teaspoon sugar
15g butter
1 tablespoon oil
4 chicken thigh fillets
1 tablespoon chopped fresh parsley

1. Add bacon, onion and garlic to frying pan, stir constantly over medium heat for 3 minutes or until onion is soft.

2. Add undrained tomatoes, water, tomato paste, dried herbs and sugar. Crush tomatoes with potato masher or fork. Bring to boil, reduce heat, simmer, uncovered, for about 10 minutes or until sauce is thick; stir occasionally during cooking time.

3. While sauce is cooking, heat butter and oil in frying pan, add chicken, cook over medium heat for about 5 minutes, or until lightly browned and tender; turn several times during cooking. Be careful not to over-cook or chicken will be dry and tough.

4. Add parsley to tomato mixture, serve over chicken with rice or pasta (see glossary).
    Serves 2.

BELOW: Pan-Fried Chicken with Tomato Bacon Sauce.

Dish: Casa Shopping; tiles: Country Floors

CHICKEN LIVERS

Chicken livers are inexpensive; buy them from a shop which is reliable, as livers tend to go stale quickly.

Chicken liver pâté makes a wonderful first course served with toast or plain savoury biscuits such as water crackers; the pâté is also good served as an appetiser with drinks.

Clarified butter is used as a seal over the surface of the pâté. This serves 2 purposes: it stops the surface from drying out and changing colour, and adds butter to the pâté while you are eating it.

CHICKEN LIVER PATE WITH PORT

Pâté is best eaten a day after it is made; this allows flavours to develop, but it will keep, covered, in refrigerator for up to a week. This recipe is not suitable to freeze.

500g chicken livers
⅓ cup port
125g butter
1 medium onion, chopped
1 clove garlic, crushed
½ teaspoon dried tarragon leaves
2 tablespoons brandy
1 tablespoon tomato paste
⅓ cup sour cream
125g butter, extra

1. Trim and wash livers, cut in half. Combine livers in small bowl with port; cover, stand 2 hours. Strain livers, melt half the butter in medium frying pan, add onion and garlic, stir constantly over medium heat for about 3 minutes or until onion is soft. Add livers to pan, stir constantly over medium heat for about 5 minutes or until livers are just changed in colour. Stir in tarragon and brandy, bring to boil, reduce heat, simmer, uncovered, for about 3 minutes or until livers are tender; do not over-cook or livers will be dry.

BELOW: Chicken Liver Pâté with Port.

Dishes: Dansab

2. Melt remaining butter in saucepan. Blend or process liver mixture until smooth, add tomato paste and sour cream, blend until combined. Add melted butter gradually while motor is operating. Pour pâté into serving dishes, garnish with sprigs of herbs or a bay leaf, if desired; cover, refrigerate for 2 hours.

3. Chop extra butter, place in small saucepan, melt over low heat, without stirring. Stand for a few minutes, then use a spoon to carefully lift off whitish coloured scum that floats on top; discard this scum. Carefully pour remaining clear liquid into jug, leaving the whitish milky deposits in the pan; discard these deposits.

4. Gently pour a thin layer of clarified butter over pâté, refrigerate overnight. Serves 4.

MICROWAVE COOKING

Cook butter, onion and garlic, uncovered, in microwave-proof dish on HIGH for about 3 minutes or until onion is soft. Add drained livers, cook on HIGH, uncovered, for about 2 minutes or until livers are just changed in colour; stir twice during cooking. Add tarragon and brandy, cook on HIGH for about 1 minute or until livers are tender. Proceed as above.

RABBIT

Rabbit is dry, lean meat and is ideal for people on low cholesterol or slimmers' diets. It is usually sold whole, although some specialty shops do sell different cuts and fillets.

OVEN-BAG COOKING

We cooked the rabbit in an oven bag, using a method that can be applied to most food suitable for roasting or casseroling. Because steam is trapped in the bag during cooking, the food is moist and tender and the flavour from the food is retained in the juices.

Oven bags are made from polyester and are designed to withstand oven temperatures up to 200 degrees Celsius (400 degrees Fahrenheit). There are several sizes available.
Follow these important tips:
● Flour should be placed in bag with food; puncture holes in bag; follow the manufacturer's instructions.
● The filled bag should be placed in a baking dish large enough to accommodate the bag completely.
● Do not have the corners of the bag hanging over the sides of the dish.

RABBIT AND BACON CASSEROLE

Rabbits are cleaned but often retain some internal organs; simply remove these and discard. Casserole can be made up to 2 days ahead; keep in bag in refrigerator. Casserole can also be frozen for up to 2 months. Recipe unsuitable to microwave.

1 rabbit
2 tablespoons oil
1 tablespoon plain flour
3 bacon rashers, coarsely chopped
1 medium onion, coarsely chopped
3 teaspoons plain flour, extra
1 tablespoon tomato paste
1 small chicken stock cube,
  crumbled
¾ cup water
⅓ cup cream

1. Remove internal organs from rabbit, cut away stomach flaps, if necessary. Cut rabbit into pieces, as shown.

2. Heat oil in medium frying pan. Gradually add rabbit to pan in single layer. Cook rabbit over high heat, turning often, for about 5 minutes or until well browned all over.

ABOVE: Rabbit and Bacon Casserole.

3. Drain rabbit on absorbent paper. Place flour in oven bag, shake well. Heat any remaining oil in pan, add bacon, cook until bacon is crisp. Add onion, cook, stirring constantly, until onion is soft. Drain bacon and onion (reserve about 1 tablespoon pan drippings), transfer to oven bag, top with rabbit pieces.

4. Stir extra flour into pan drippings in pan, cook, stirring constantly, over high heat until mixture browns slightly. Remove from heat. Gradually stir in combined tomato paste, stock cube and water. Return to heat, stir constantly over high heat until mixture boils and thickens, stir in cream. Add sauce to oven bag, seal bag, puncture 3 or 4 holes in bag near the sealed end, place in baking dish, bake in moderate oven for about 1 hour or until rabbit is tender.
Serves 2.

SALADS

Salads have become accepted as part of many different types of meals as well as being used as entrées or main courses. When a salad is used as a main course, it often has ingredients such as meat, seafood, chicken, egg or cheese added to make it more substantial.

We have used tossed green leafy salads as an accompaniment to many of our recipes throughout this book. Use whatever green salad vegetables you like. As a rule, the cheapest are at the peak of their season. Try a variety of mixed lettuce. The slightly bitter red radicchio goes well with the good old-fashioned iceberg, also with the pretty mignonette, lamb's ear or butter lettuce. The addition of witlof, endive, watercress, young spinach or silverbeet all add interest, texture and different tastes to salads. There are many other types of vegetables suitable to add to the leafy ones. For example, onions, radishes, green shallots, cucumbers, peppers, celery, cabbage, tomatoes, etc. It is important to wash and dry all vegetables well, but particularly the soft leafy ones. These can be dried by tea-towels, then stored in airtight plastic bags or containers in the refrigerator. Or, water can be spun out of the vegetables by using a lettuce dryer. These work very efficiently by centrifugal force. They are obtainable from stores which sell kitchen equipment. There are plastic containers designed specifically for storing lettuce. Wash the lettuce first, drain, remove core and place lettuce in container; secure lid.

It is important to remember to add the dressing to the salad just before serving, or the salad will be limp and soggy. You can use French dressing, either home-made (see recipe in Rice Salad with French Dressing) or bottled. Use only a little, just enough to barely coat the vegetables. Toss ingredients together lightly using your hands (best for a lot of salad) or use salad servers.

TABBOULEH

Tabbouleh or tabbouli is a delicious salad from Lebanon; it can be eaten with meat dishes and makes wonderful portable food in a pita bread pocket or hollowed-out bread roll.

Tabbouleh's two main ingredients are parsley, which gives a slightly astringent flavour, and burghul, also known as bulgur or cracked wheat. This needs no cooking but is soaked in boiling water then drained and blotted on absorbent paper. It is important to blot as much water as possible from burghul to give a chewy texture.

The recipe should be made using Continental parsley; it has large, flat leaves. These and the stalks should be chopped as evenly as possible. You can use the regular curly-leafed parsley, if you prefer, but it tends to turn a little mushy and, of course, the flavour is different.

TASTY TABBOULEH

You will need to buy about 2 bunches Continental parsley and 1 bunch mint for this recipe. Burghul is available from health food stores and some supermarkets. Tabbouleh can be made 2 days ahead; keep, covered, in refrigerator. This recipe is not suitable to freeze.

½ cup burghul
2 small tomatoes
5 green shallots
1 small onion
1½ cups chopped fresh mint
4 cups chopped fresh
   Continental parsley
1½ tablespoons oil
1½ tablespoons lemon juice

1. Place burghul in small bowl, cover with boiling water, stand 15 minutes. While burghul is soaking, chop tomatoes, shallots and onion.

2. Drain burghul well in fine strainer, rinse under cold water, drain well, then blot moisture using absorbent paper.

3. Combine all ingredients in large bowl, mix gently.
   Serves 6.

RIGHT: Tasty Tabbouleh.

Bowl: Dansab; background: Wilson Fabrics

COLESLAW

This recipe for coleslaw is a basic one to which you can add many other ingredients to suit your taste (coleslaw is a cabbage salad). Peppers, celery and onion are good additions; however, onion is best added just before serving as it doesn't keep well.

You can use any type of cabbage; the traditional one is the firm, white drumhead cabbage; the curly Savoy or even Chinese cabbage will also give good results. Slice cabbage as finely as you like.

Use a commercially-made or home-made mayonnaise of your choice (see Waldorf Salad for how to make the mayonnaise).

CRISP COLESLAW

Coleslaw can be made up to 3 days ahead; keep, covered, in refrigerator. This recipe is not suitable to freeze or microwave.

½ **small cabbage**
1 medium carrot, grated
4 green shallots, chopped
¼ cup mayonnaise
2 teaspoons lemon juice
1. Using sharp knife, remove core from cabbage; shred cabbage finely.

2. Combine cabbage, carrot and shallots in large bowl, add combined mayonnaise and lemon juice, mix well.
Serves 4.

ABOVE: Crisp Coleslaw.

Bowl: Dansab; background fabric: Balmain Linen & Lace

POTATO SALAD

Potatoes mixed lightly with mayonnaise are the basis of this popular salad; we added an egg to make it even tastier. We like to use a firm potato such as Pontiac or Kennebec. However, if you prefer, new potatoes are delicious. These can be boiled or steamed with their skins left on, then peeled while they are still hot, or serve them skins and all.

Potatoes can be cooked and cut up while they are hot, but, for easier handling, we prefer to cut up raw potatoes then cook them. Take care not to over-cook the potato cubes or they will become too soft and crumbly and spoil the look of the salad.

You can use a commercial or home-made mayonnaise (see Waldorf Salad for mayonnaise recipe). Potato salad is delicious served either hot or cold.

POTATO SALAD WITH EGG AND SHALLOTS

Salad can be prepared up to 2 days ahead; keep, covered, in refrigerator. Recipe unsuitable to freeze.

500g potatoes
1 hard-boiled egg, chopped
½ cup mayonnaise
2 teaspoons white vinegar
2 green shallots, chopped
2 teaspoons chopped fresh parsley

1. Peel potatoes, cut into cubes as large or as small as you like; keep them as even as possible.

2. Half-fill medium saucepan with hot water, cover, bring to boil, add potatoes, return to boil, reduce heat, simmer for about 5 minutes or until potatoes are just tender when pierced with skewer. Pour into strainer carefully to prevent potatoes breaking, immediately spread on oven tray to cool. If serving salad hot, transfer to large bowl and add the prepared mayonnaise mixture.

3. Combine egg, mayonnaise and vinegar in blender or processor, blend or process until smooth. Combine potatoes, mayonnaise mixture, shallots and parsley in bowl, mix gently to coat potatoes evenly.

Serves 2.

MICROWAVE COOKING

Place potato cubes in a shallow microwave-proof dish with 2 tablespoons water, cover, cook on HIGH for about 10 minutes or until potatoes are just tender; stir potatoes several times during cooking.

BELOW: Potato Salad with Egg and Shallots.

Dish: Lifestyle Imports; tiles: Pazotti

RICE SALAD

Cold rice mixes deliciously with many other ingredients to make tempting and satisfying salads; these are perfect for family meals, picnics, packed lunches or special occasions.

You can use any of the different types of white and brown rice. We cooked rice freshly (see glossary) but left-over rice is also suitable.

RICE SALAD WITH FRENCH DRESSING

Salad can be made a day ahead; keep, covered, in refrigerator. Add dressing just before serving. Recipe unsuitable to freeze.

1 cup rice
4 green shallots, finely chopped
1 medium red pepper, finely chopped
310g can corn niblets, drained
450g can pineapple pieces, drained
⅓ cup sultanas
FRENCH DRESSING
⅓ cup oil
2 tablespoons white vinegar or lemon juice
¼ teaspoon dry mustard
¼ teaspoon sugar

1. Add rice to large saucepan of boiling water, boil rapidly, uncovered, for about 12 minutes or until tender. Drain rice, rinse under cold water, drain well. Combine rice with remaining ingredients in large bowl, mix well.

2. French Dressing: Combine oil, vinegar, mustard and sugar in screw-top jar; shake well to combine ingredients. Add dressing to rice mixture, mix well.

Serves 6.

BEAN SALAD

Beans are incredibly rich in dietary fibre and are really good in salads. Many varieties are available; they can be mixed to suit your taste. Add interest with crunchy and colourful vegetables and a tangy dressing (see French Dressing, left).

Beans can be freshly cooked (see glossary) or canned; we like canned beans as they are convenient and time-saving. Rinse canned beans well under cold running water and drain well before using.

QUICK BEAN SALAD

Salad can be made up to 3 days ahead; keep, covered, in refrigerator. Recipe unsuitable to freeze.

310g can red kidney beans
310g can butter (cannellini) beans
310g can four bean mix
1 stick celery, chopped
1 small onion, sliced
1 long thin green cucumber, sliced
1 tablespoon oil
2 tablespoons French dressing
1 tablespoon chopped fresh parsley
1 teaspoon dry mustard
1 tablespoon lemon juice
½ teaspoon grated fresh ginger

1. Place beans in strainer, rinse well under cold running water; drain well.

2. Combine beans, celery, onion and cucumber in medium bowl. Pour over combined oil, dressing, parsley, mustard, lemon juice and ginger; mix lightly until well combined.

Serves 6.

LEFT: Top: Rice Salad with French Dressing; bottom: Quick Bean Salad.

Dishes: Dansab; background: Abet Laminati

PASTA SALAD

Pasta salad is a good accompaniment to meat; it is very popular served at a barbecue. Use the size, shape and colour of pasta you prefer or mix several types together for a more interesting appearance; see glossary for more information on cooking pasta.

The slightly sweet curry dressing we have used looks and tastes great with pasta. However, you can increase the curry powder if you want it hotter.

CURRIED PASTA SALAD

Salad can be prepared up to 2 days ahead; keep, covered, in refrigerator. This recipe is not suitable to freeze or microwave.

1 cup pasta
1 medium red pepper, chopped
1 medium green pepper, chopped
2 tablespoons chopped fresh chives
100g baby mushrooms, chopped

CURRY DRESSING
2 teaspoons curry powder
1 tablespoon castor sugar
½ cup oil
¼ cup white vinegar
1 tablespoon cream
1. Bring large saucepan of water to the boil, gradually add pasta. Boil rapidly, uncovered, for about 10 minutes or until pasta is tender; drain well. Place into large bowl with peppers, chives and mushrooms.

ABOVE: Curried Pasta Salad.

Bowl: Villa Italiana; tiles: Northbridge Ceramic and Marble Centre

2. Curry Dressing: Combine curry powder and sugar in small bowl, gradually stir in oil, vinegar and cream.
Serves 4.

WALDORF

Waldorf Salad is an American recipe. The crunchy apple, celery and nuts are always lightly bound together with a mayonnaise. If you don't want to make your own mayonnaise, use a good-quality commercially-made mayonnaise of your choice.

Mayonnaise is easy to make if you do exactly as directed. The main problem of curdling occurs when the oil is added too quickly.

If this happens, remove the curdled mixture from the blender or processor to a jug. Place another egg yolk into the blender or processor, add the curdled mixture drop by drop while the motor is operating. Once the mixture is holding together, add the rest of the curdled mixture in a thin stream while the motor is operating.

WALDORF SALAD WITH HOME-MADE MAYONNAISE

Use half the quantity of mayonnaise for this recipe, keep remaining mayonnaise, covered, in refrigerator for up to a week. This recipe is not suitable to freeze.

2 large apples, coarsely chopped
2 sticks celery, sliced
½ cup pecans or walnuts
1 tablespoon lemon juice
MAYONNAISE
2 egg yolks
1 teaspoon dry mustard
2 teaspoons lemon juice
1 cup oil
2 tablespoons hot water, approximately
Combine apples, celery, nuts and lemon juice in bowl.

Mayonnaise: Blend or process egg yolks, mustard and juice until smooth. Add oil gradually in a thin stream while motor is operating; stir in enough hot water to give a pouring consistency. Stir through apple mixture.

Serves 4.

BELOW: Waldorf Salad with Home-Made Mayonnaise.

Tiles: Northbridge Ceramic & Marble Centre

SOUPS

There is nothing quite so satisfying as home-made soup. Serve it as a first course, a snack, or as a main meal with crusty bread, toast, crumpets or muffins. In this section we have included a smart tomato soup which can be served hot or cold, a puréed vegetable soup, a good old-fashioned beef and vegetable soup and a quick and easy chicken soup that needs minimal preparation.

BEEF

This, is a good old-fashioned soup thickened slightly by the addition of barley. You can use rice, white or brown, if you prefer.

The flavour of this soup is better if it is made a day before it is required. Cool it to room temperature, then transfer it to a large jar or bowl. Cover, refrigerate overnight.

Any fat can be lifted from the soup before it is reheated.

HEARTY BEEF AND VEGETABLE SOUP

Recipe can be made up to 2 days ahead; keep, covered, in refrigerator or freeze for up to 2 months. This recipe is not suitable to microwave.

500g gravy beef
2 medium onions, chopped
1 medium carrot, chopped
2 sticks celery, chopped
1 small swede, chopped
1 medium parsnip, chopped
¼ cup pearl barley
1 litre (4 cups) water
2 small beef stock cubes, crumbled

Trim any fat from beef, chop beef into 2cm cubes. Combine beef, onions, carrot, celery, swede, parsnip and pearl barley in large saucepan, add water and stock cubes. Bring to boil, reduce heat, cover, simmer for 1½ hours or until beef is tender.
Serves 4

ABOVE: Hearty Beef and Vegetable Soup.

2. Melt butter in large saucepan, add onion and bacon, stir constantly over heat until onion is soft.

3. Add pumpkin to pan, then water and stock cube, bring to boil, reduce heat, cover, simmer for about 30 minutes or until pumpkin is tender.

4. Remove saucepan from heat. Blend or process mixture in several batches until smooth. Return mixture to pan, stir in cream; reheat, stirring constantly without boiling.

Serves 4.

PUMPKIN

Any type of pumpkin can be used in this recipe, but we like the older style for a more savoury flavour. The softer butternut and golden nugget pumpkins tend to give a sweeter-flavoured soup.

PUMPKIN CREAM SOUP

Soup can be made a day ahead; keep, covered, in refrigerator. Soup can also be frozen, without cream, for up to 2 months. Add cream when reheating over low heat.

750g pumpkin
15g butter
1 medium onion, chopped
2 bacon rashers, chopped
1 litre (4 cups) water

1 small chicken stock cube, crumbled
¼ cup cream

1. Using sharp knife, remove skin and seeds from pumpkin, cut into small even pieces.

MICROWAVE COOKING

Unpeeled pumpkin can be microwaved for a minute or 2 (the time depends on the size of the pieces), then peeled quite easily with a knife. Combine butter, onion and bacon in large shallow microwave-proof dish, cover, cook on HIGH for about 3 minutes or until onion is soft. Add pumpkin, water and stock cube, cover, cook on HIGH for about 15 minutes or until pumpkin is tender. Proceed as above.

ABOVE LEFT: Pumpkin Cream Soup.

TOMATO

This soup is delicious provided the tomatoes are flavoursome. If the regular tomatoes are bland, try using the egg-shaped variety or the small cherry or Tom Thumb. These are reliably full of taste. If using cherry tomatoes, cook them with the peel and strain before serving.

We have left this soup only partly processed and unstrained to give a coarse texture. You can process it until it is as smooth as you like, then strain it, if you prefer.

This type of soup can be served hot or cold; swirl in a little cream, sour cream, light sour cream or yoghurt just before serving, if you prefer.

FRESH TOMATO SOUP

Soup can be prepared up to 2 days ahead; keep, covered, in refrigerator. Soup can be frozen for up to 2 months.

500g tomatoes
2 tablespoons oil
1 clove garlic, finely chopped
1 medium onion, coarsely chopped
1 tablespoon tomato paste
1 bay leaf
1 small chicken stock cube,
  crumbled
⅔ cup water
½ teaspoon whole black
  peppercorns

1. Using a sharp knife, carefully remove cores from tomatoes, cut small crosses at opposite ends. Place tomatoes in medium saucepan with enough boiling water to cover tomatoes. Boil for about 30 seconds; strain immediately, place into bowl of iced water, peel away skin.

2. Chop tomatoes roughly.

3. Heat oil in medium saucepan. Add garlic and onion, stir over heat for 3 minutes. Add tomatoes then remaining ingredients. Bring to boil, reduce heat

cover, simmer 25 minutes. Discard bay leaf; blend or process mixture.
Serves 4.

MICROWAVE COOKING

Combine oil, garlic and onion in microwave-proof dish, cook, uncovered, on HIGH for 3 minutes. Add the remaining ingredients, cook on HIGH, uncovered, for 15 minutes and proceed as above.

BELOW: Fresh Tomato Soup.

Bowl & plate: Villa Italiana

1. Combine water, stock cube, ginger, onion and parsley in medium saucepan with chicken. Bring to boil, reduce heat, cover, simmer for about 10 minutes or until chicken is tender. Strain stock, reserve chicken.

2. Return stock to saucepan, add corn and extra ginger, bring to boil. Blend cornflour with extra water in small bowl, add to stock, stir constantly over heat until mixture boils and thickens.

3. Chop cooked chicken, add to corn mixture with ham and shallot. Reheat before serving, if necessary.
Serves 4.

MICROWAVE COOKING
Add ingredients for stock with chicken to large, shallow microwave-proof dish, cook, covered, on HIGH for about 5 minutes or until chicken is tender. Strain, reserve chicken, return stock to dish with corn, extra ginger, blended cornflour and extra water. Cook on HIGH for about 2 minutes, stirring occasionally, or until mixture boils and thickens. Proceed as above.

CHICKEN

This tasty soup is quick and easy with minimal chopping of ingredients and no need to purée the mixture. It uses convenient stock cubes and canned food. Soup is best served immediately it is made.

CHICKEN AND CORN SOUP

Soup can be made up to a day ahead; keep, covered, in refrigerator. Recipe unsuitable to freeze.

2 cups water
1 small chicken stock cube, crumbled
1 teaspoon grated fresh ginger
1 small onion, sliced
4 parsley sprigs
4 chicken thigh fillets
2 x 130g cans creamed corn
½ teaspoon grated fresh ginger, extra
1 tablespoon cornflour
1 tablespoon water, extra
60g ham, sliced
1 green shallot, chopped

ABOVE LEFT: Chicken and Corn Soup.

PASTA

Macaroni is the generic term for all types of pasta, and Italy is credited with perfecting the art of cooking it. Most macaronis have Italian names; when translated, they describe the pasta. For example, spaghetti means little strings. Pasta is made basically from flour and eggs and comes in many shapes and flavours. It gives you energy and is not fattening by itself. It can be fresh, frozen or dried (see glossary for cooking details). All can be served with these 4 delicious sauces. If you need to feed quite a lot of people, sauces can be made ahead of serving time, then reheated and served over freshly-cooked pasta.

1. Heat oil in large saucepan, add onion and garlic, stir constantly over medium heat for about 5 minutes or until soft.

2. Add mince to pan, stir constantly over high heat until well browned.

3. Add undrained tomatoes, tomato paste, water, stock cube, sugar and herbs, crush tomatoes with potato masher or fork. Bring to boil, reduce heat, cover, simmer for about 30 minutes or until mince is tender and mixture thickened slightly. Serve over hot pasta.

Serves 4.

MEAT SAUCE

Bolognese sauce makes a favourite standard meal served over spaghetti or any pasta. It is easy to make, tasty and economical. Cook 375g pasta to accompany this sauce; serve as a snack or as a hearty meal for 4 topped with grated parmesan cheese; add a tossed salad and crusty bread.

ABOVE: Bolognese Sauce.

Bowl: Villa Italiana

BOLOGNESE SAUCE

Sauce can be made 3 days ahead; keep, covered, in refrigerator, or freeze for 2 months. Recipe unsuitable to microwave.

1 tablespoon oil
1 medium onion, finely chopped
1 clove garlic, crushed
500g minced beef
410g can tomatoes
¼ cup tomato paste
¼ cup water
1 small beef stock cube, crumbled
½ teaspoon sugar
¼ teaspoon dried basil leaves
¼ teaspoon dried oregano leaves

...matoes for
...you can use
...(see glossary)
...refer. Cook 375g
...y this robust sauce.
...are best served as a
h...

TOMA... WITH RED WINE SAUCE

Sauce can be prepared up to a day ahead; add herbs just before serving. Sauce can be frozen for 2 months.

30g butter
1 medium onion, chopped
1 clove garlic, crushed
410g can tomatoes
¼ cup dry red wine
¼ cup water
2 teaspoons tomato paste
1 small chicken stock cube, crumbled
1 teaspoon cornflour
1 tablespoon water, extra
1 teaspoon sugar
2 teaspoons chopped fresh basil
1 tablespoon chopped fresh parsley

1. Melt butter in frying pan, add onion and garlic, stir constantly over medium heat until onion is soft. Add undrained crushed tomatoes, wine, water, tomato paste and stock cube, bring to boil, reduce heat, simmer, uncovered, for 10 minutes.

2. Stir in blended cornflour and extra water, stir constantly over high heat until mixture boils and thickens. Stir in sugar and herbs. Serve tomato sauce over hot pasta.
   Serves 4.

MICROWAVE COOKING

Cook butter, onion and garlic in microwave-proof dish, uncovered, on HIGH for about 3 minutes or until onion is soft. Add tomatoes, as above, cook on HIGH for 10 minutes. Proceed as above, cook on HIGH for about 2 minutes or until mixture boils and thickens. Stir twice during cooking.

HERB SAUCE

Pesto is wonderfully flavoured with fresh, peppery basil. You don't need a lot of this sauce over pasta; cook 375g pasta for this quantity of pesto sauce. Serve sauce and pasta as a main course for 4 or an entree for 8.

PESTO SAUCE

We used olive oil in this recipe, but any oil can be used. Pesto sauce can be prepared up to a week ahead; keep, covered, in refrigerator. Sauce can be frozen for 3 months. Recipe unsuitable to microwave.

15g butter
¼ cup pine nuts
1 cup fresh basil leaves, firmly packed
1 clove garlic, crushed
2 tablespoons grated parmesan cheese
1 teaspoon sugar
½ cup olive oil

1. Melt butter in small saucepan, add pine nuts, stir constantly over medium heat until nuts are browned; cool.

2. Process basil with pine nuts, garlic, cheese and sugar until smooth.

3. Add oil gradually in a thin stream while motor is operating, process until combined. Serve over hot pasta.
   Serves 4.

Clockwise from left: Pesto Sauce; Tomato with Red Wine Sauce; Creamy Ham and Mushroom Sauce.

Bowls: Villa Italiana; tiles: Northbridge Ceramic & Marble Centre

CREAMY SAUCE

Cream is a rich and delicious add[...] to this sauce; you can boil the cream[...] the sauce because it contains flour. Cook 375g pasta to accompany this sauce to make a meal for 4. It would also make a delicious entrée for 8.

CREAMY HAM AND MUSHROOM SAUCE

Sauce can be prepared up to a day ahead. Add mushrooms, ham and pepper just before reheating. Recipe unsuitable to freeze or microwave.

30g butter
185g mushrooms, sliced
15g butter, extra
1 tablespoon plain flour
½ small chicken stock cube,
   crumbled
1 cup milk
½ cup cream
¼ cup dry white wine
200g ham, chopped
1 medium red pepper, thinly sliced

1. Melt butter in frying pan, add mushrooms, stir constantly over medium heat for about 3 minutes or until mushrooms are soft. Remove mushrooms from pan.

2. Add extra butter to the same pan, stir in flour and stock cube, stir constantly over medium heat for about 1 minute or until mixture is bubbly. Stir in milk, cream and wine, stir constantly over high heat until sauce mixture boils and thickens.

3. Stir in ham, mushrooms and pepper, cook for about 3 minutes to heat through. Serve over hot pasta.
   Serves 4.

MACARONI

Macaroni with cheesy white sauce is one of those "comfort foods". It is soft and tasty to eat. Any left-over vegetables can be added as well as the peas or instead of them. Eggs can be left out, if you prefer. Well-drained salmon or tuna, or ham or chicken can be added to make it more hearty.

MACARONI CHEESE

Use fresh or dehydrated peas and cook them before using, or use left-over cooked peas or thawed frozen peas. The heat from the sauce will be enough to tenderise frozen peas. This dish can be prepared up to 2 days ahead; keep, covered, in refrigerator. This recipe is unsuitable to freeze.

1 cup macaroni
30g butter
2 tablespoons plain flour
2 teaspoons dry mustard
1½ cups milk
¾ cup grated tasty cheese
2 hard-boiled eggs, quartered
½ cup peas
2 tablespoons chopped fresh parsley

1. Bring large saucepan of water to boil, gradually add macaroni, boil, uncovered, for about 12 minutes or until macaroni is tender; drain well.

2. Melt butter in large saucepan, stir in flour and mustard. Stir constantly over medium heat for about 2 minutes or until mixture is bubbly; do not allow mixture to brown.

3. Remove from heat, gradually stir in milk. Return to heat, stir constantly over medium heat until the sauce boils and thickens slightly.

4. Add cheese, stir until melted.

5. Gently stir in macaroni, eggs, peas and parsley. Serve immediately or place in heatproof dish, sprinkle top with a little extra cheese, place under hot griller for a few minutes or until lightly browned. You can also place mixture in ovenproof dish and bake, uncovered, in moderate oven for about 20 minutes or until lightly browned and heated through.
   Serves 4.

MICROWAVE COOKING

Melt butter in large microwave-proof dish on HIGH for about 1 minute; stir in flour and mustard then milk gradually. Cook on HIGH, uncovered, for about 3 minutes or until mixture boils and thickens. Stir several times during the cooking. Add cheese, stir until melted, then add remaining ingredients.

LEFT: Macaroni Cheese.

Plate: Incorporated Agencies

RICE

Rice is one of the great grains of the world and, though it has no decided flavour on its own, it does wonders for all kinds of dishes both savoury and sweet. You can choose many types of white or brown rice; all are wholesome, although some people prefer brown rice because it is more nutritious and has a slightly chewy texture. Rice can be mixed into a dish or served as an accompaniment. It has great value as a meal extender for you need only a little meat, chicken or seafood plus a tasty sauce to make a nutritious, satisfying dish. By cooking it our way, you will get perfect results every time (see glossary).

FRIED RICE

There are several methods of making fried rice. This is the easiest because it uses already-cooked rice. Fried rice can be used as an accompaniment to meat or other Chinese-style dishes. It can be made into a main meal by adding a variety of other ingredients.

Small pieces of any type of cooked meat, poultry or seafood can be added to the wok with the cooked rice. Chicken, ham, bacon, pork, beef and prawns are among the most popular.

A wok is ideal for cooking fried rice, but a large frying pan, manual or electric, will also do the job well. (See Sweet and Sour Pork for more information about wok cookery.)

EASY FRIED RICE

This dish is best made just before serving. This recipe is not suitable to freeze or microwave.

1 tablespoon oil
½ teaspoon sesame oil
2 eggs, lightly beaten
1 clove garlic, finely chopped
½ teaspoon grated fresh ginger
3 green shallots, chopped
1 small red pepper, chopped
100g baby mushrooms, sliced
1 stick celery, sliced
130g can corn kernels, drained
2 teaspoons light soy sauce
3 cups cooked rice

1. Heat both oils in wok or large frying pan, transfer oils to small bowl; reserve oils. Gradually pour eggs into wok, tilting so that eggs cover base, continue to cook until eggs are set. Transfer this omelet to large plate to cool before chopping.

over high heat for about 1 minute or until vegetables are almost tender.
3. Add soy sauce, rice and chopped omelet. Stir-fry constantly for about 2 minutes over high heat or until mixture is heated through.
Serves 4.

ABOVE RIGHT: Easy Fried Rice.

Bowl, chopsticks and rest: Made Where; table: The Country Trader

2. Return reserved oils to wok, add garlic, ginger, shallots, pepper, mushrooms, celery and corn. Stir-fry

COOKING RICE BY ABSORPTION

The famous Italian rice dish, risotto, can include many different types of meat, vegetables and flavourings to vary the taste. For example, wine can replace some of the water or stock. Garlic, celery, mushrooms, peppers, zucchini, bacon and chicken, etc, can all be added.

Cooked risotto should be slightly moist and creamy in texture, and is usually served by itself. This method of cooking rice is like the steamed method, where the moisture is absorbed by the rice (see glossary).

TOMATO RISOTTO

Prepare risotto as close to serving time as possible. Recipe unsuitable to freeze or microwave.

2 medium tomatoes, peeled
45g butter
1 small onion, finely chopped
½ cup long grain rice
1½ cups water
1 small chicken stock cube,
    crumbled
1 bay leaf
2 teaspoons chopped fresh basil
2 tablespoons grated parmesan
    cheese

1. Peel tomatoes (see glossary). Cut tomatoes in half, remove seeds from each half by gently squeezing or using a teaspoon (see glossary). Chop tomatoes finely.

2. Melt butter in medium saucepan, add onion, stir constantly over medium heat until onion is soft. Add rice to pan, mix well to coat each grain with butter.

3. Stir in tomatoes, water, stock cube and bay leaf. Stir constantly over medium heat for about 20 minutes or until almost all the water has been absorbed. Rice should still be quite moist at this stage.

4. Remove pan from heat, stir in basil and cheese. Sprinkle with extra parmesan cheese, if desired.
    Serves 2.

TOP: Tomato Risotto.

Dish: Studio-Haus; tiles: Pazotti

CREAMED RICE

Creamed rice is another old-fashioned favourite; eat it by itself or with fresh, canned or home-stewed fruit. It can be served hot or cold.

If you prefer it cold, cook for only about half the time or until two-thirds of the milk has been absorbed. By the time the rice has cooled, it will have absorbed the remaining milk.

CREAMED RICE WITH STEWED APPLES

We used Granny Smith apples in this recipe. Recipe unsuitable to freeze or microwave.

½ cup short grain rice
1 litre (4 cups) milk
½ cup sugar
1 teaspoon vanilla essence
STEWED APPLES
2 apples
½ cup water
1 tablespoon sugar

1. Wash rice well in strainer under cold running water, drain well. Combine milk and sugar in medium heavy-based saucepan, bring to boil, add rice, reduce heat to as low as possible, cover with tight-fitting lid. Rice must be cooked gently, just barely simmering, or it will burn on the base of the pan.

2. Cook for about 1 hour; stir several times during cooking time to make sure rice has not stuck to base of saucepan. Cook until almost all of the milk has been absorbed. Add essence, serve hot with stewed apples, sprinkle with cinnamon, if desired.

3. Stewed Apples: Peel, quarter, core and slice apples. Bring water and sugar to boil in medium saucepan, add apples. Cover, return to boil, reduce heat, simmer, covered, for about

5 minutes or until apples are just tender. Apples can be drained or served with the syrup.

Serves 4.

MICROWAVE COOKING OF APPLES

Combine water and sugar in microwave-proof dish, cover, cook on HIGH for about 1 minute or until mixture comes to boil. Add prepared apples, cover, cook on HIGH for about 3 minutes or until apples are just tender. Proceed as above.

TOP: Creamed Rice.

Bowl: Incorporated Agencies

PASTRY

Pastry is easy to make and handle with just a little practice. In this section, we show you how to make a good, rich shortcrust pastry which can be used for sweet and savoury fillings. There is also a favourite simple pastry for sweet pies. Fillo pastry, bought in packets of very fine sheets, requires just a few tips for best handling; it is quick and crispy for sweet and savoury fillings.

RICH SHORTCRUST PASTRY

Rich shortcrust pastry is one of the most used of all pastries; it should be handled quickly and lightly at all times. Over-handling will make it tough and dry, and difficult to roll out.

Only the minimum amount of liquid should be used to make the ingredients cling together; too-soft pastry will shrink during cooking. If you mix the pastry in a food processor you need slightly less liquid than if it is made by hand.

BAKING BLIND

The method of cooking called "baking blind" is used in this recipe. The pastry is placed into the tin but it is cooked without any filling; you weigh it down with dried beans, peas or rice on baking or greaseproof paper (see glossary).

"Baking blind" ensures a crisp pastry case, especially when using a "wet" filling as with a quiche.

QUICHE LORRAINE

Swiss or a tasty cheddar cheese can be used in place of gruyere, if preferred. Pastry cases can be cooked up to a week ahead; keep in airtight container. This recipe is not suitable to freeze or microwave.

RICH SHORTCRUST PASTRY
1 cup plain flour
90g butter
1 egg yolk
3 teaspoons lemon juice
FILLING
3 bacon rashers, chopped
60g gruyere cheese, sliced
3 green shallots, finely chopped
1 egg
½ cup cream

FAR RIGHT: Quiche Lorraine.

Plate, rack, spoon & tea-towel: Australian East India Co.

1. Rich Shortcrust Pastry: Sift flour into medium bowl, rub in butter with fingertips or process in food processor until just combined.

2. Add egg yolk and enough lemon juice to make ingredients cling together when pressed lightly with your fingertips (or in processor).

3. Turn onto lightly floured surface, knead gently until smooth. Wrap in plastic wrap; refrigerate 30 minutes.

4. Roll out pastry on lightly floured surface, large enough to fit 2 x 10cm flan tins. Cut pastry in half, carefully lift pastry into each tin, gently ease into tins, do not stretch pastry. Press pastry into fluted sides. Cover pastry with greaseproof or baking paper,

place about ½ cup dried peas, beans or rice into each tin. Place tins on oven tray, bake in moderately hot oven for 7 minutes. Remove paper and beans, bake pastry cases further 7 minutes or until lightly browned, cool to room temperature before using.

5. Filling: Cook bacon in small frying pan over medium heat until crisp; drain on absorbent paper. Cover pastry bases with cheese, sprinkle evenly with bacon and shallots.

6. Combine egg and cream in small bowl, beat until combined. Divide egg mixture evenly between quiches. Bake in moderate oven for about 20 minutes or until set and lightly browned.
Serves 2.

PASTRY

pastry is obtainable from delicatessens and most supermarkets. Some is refrigerated and some frozen; both are good products provided they have been handled properly between the time they leave the manufacturer and the time they reach the refrigerator or freezer of the supermarket.

Once fillo has been opened it will keep for a while in the refrigerator; check the individual manufacturer's instructions for proper storage.

It is important to keep fillo covered while handling, as the thin sheets tend to dry out and break up. We found the most effective way is to cover the pastry completely with a piece of plastic wrap or greaseproof paper, then a well-wrung-out, damp tea-towel.

SPINACH PIE

Spinach pie can be served hot or cold, as an entrée or lunch dish. Recipe unsuitable to freeze or microwave.

**8 medium spinach (silver beet)
   leaves**
30g butter
6 green shallots, chopped
½ cup cottage cheese
150g feta cheese, crumbled
⅓ cup grated parmesan cheese
¼ teaspoon ground nutmeg
4 eggs, lightly beaten
8 sheets fillo pastry
60g butter, melted, extra

1. Wash spinach thoroughly, pat dry, trim away stems. Place spinach in large saucepan, cover, bring to boil, reduce heat, simmer, covered, for about 3 minutes or until spinach is tender. Pour into colander or strainer to drain; cool to room temperature. Squeeze out as much excess liquid as you can; use your hand to do this. Chop spinach finely, place in medium bowl.

Heat butter in small frying pan, add shallots, cook over medium heat for about 3 minutes or until shallots are soft. Add to spinach with cheeses, nutmeg and eggs, stir well.

2. Unfold pastry from packet, carefully remove 8 sheets, wrap pastry and return to packet. Place the 8 sheets flat on the bench, cover as described above. Place 1 of these sheets separately on bench, brush with some of the extra butter. Place another layer on first sheet, brush with butter. Repeat layers with 2 more sheets of pastry and butter.

3. Grease 13cm x 23cm ovenproof dish. Place the 4 joined sheets carefully into dish, trim pastry with scissors about 2cm from the edge of dish. Spread spinach mixture evenly into dish; do not press down.

4. Layer remaining 4 sheets pastry with some of the remaining butter, fold pastry in half. Lightly moisten edges of pastry in dish with water, place folded pastry on top of spinach mixture, trim edges, if necessary, to fit dish. Gently fold edges of pastry together, brush top with butter. Bake in moderately hot oven for about 40 minutes, or until golden brown.

RIGHT: Spinach Pie.

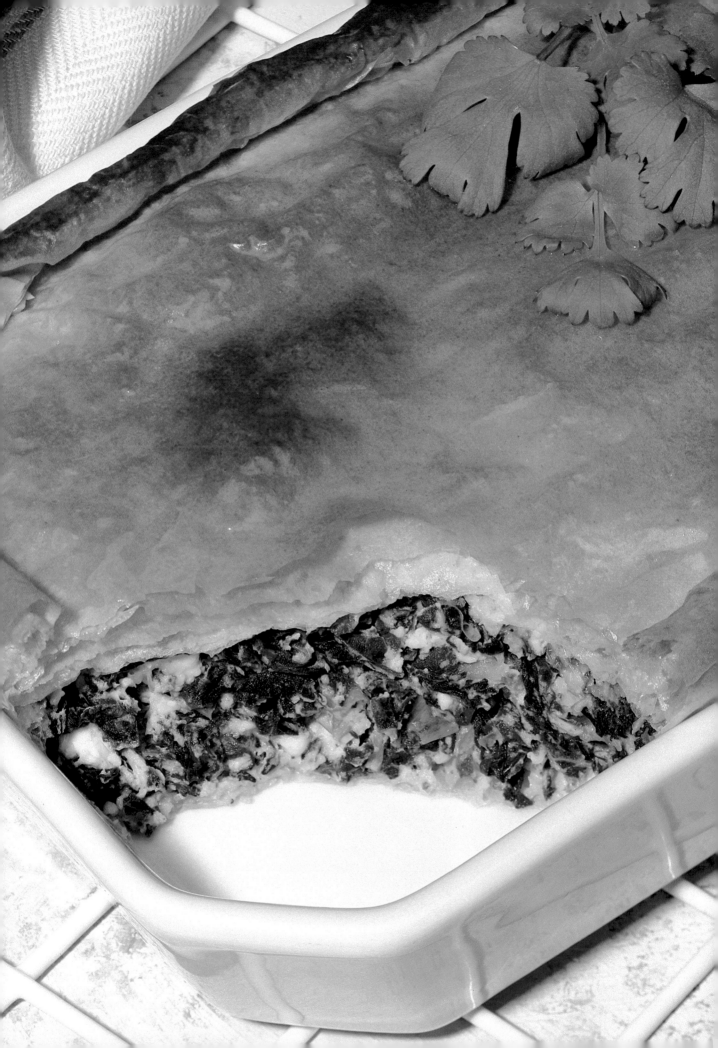

SIMPLE SWEET PASTRY

This pastry is a soft, biscuity type using a little raising agent. The method of rubbing in the butter is similar to the method for making shortcrust pastry. This pastry is easy for the beginner cook to handle.

You do not need to grease the pie plate for this pastry, as the mixture contains enough butter to prevent it from sticking to the plate.

You can serve the apple pie warm or cold with cream and/or ice-cream.

OLD-FASHIONED APPLE PIE

Pie can be made 2 days ahead, but pastry will tend to soften a little under the apple. Keep pie, covered, in refrigerator. Pastry can be made a day ahead; wrap in plastic wrap, keep in refrigerator. Pastry can be frozen for 2 months. Allow pastry to return to room temperature before rolling out to required size. Uncooked pie can be frozen for up to 2 months. This recipe is not suitable to microwave.

PASTRY
1 cup plain flour
½ cup self-raising flour
¼ cup cornflour
¼ cup custard powder
1 tablespoon castor sugar
125g butter, chopped
1 egg, separated
¼ cup water, approximately
1 tablespoon castor sugar, extra
LEMONY APPLE FILLING
7 large apples
½ cup water
2 tablespoons sugar
¼ teaspoon ground cinnamon
1 teaspoon grated lemon rind

1. Pastry: Combine sifted flours, custard powder and sugar in large bowl, rub in chopped butter with fingertips or process in food processor until ingredients are just combined.

RIGHT: Old-Fashioned Apple Pie.

Whisk and sifter: The Bay Tree

2. Add enough combined egg yolk and water to mix to a firm dough. This can also be done in food processor. Turn dough onto lightly floured surface, knead gently until smooth (see glossary). Cut dough in half, wrap in plastic wrap, refrigerate 30 minutes.

Roll out half the pastry between sheets of plastic wrap or greaseproof paper until large enough to line deep 23cm pie plate.

3. Remove top piece of plastic from pastry. Use remaining plastic to help turn pastry into pie plate. Carefully press pastry into pie plate; do not stretch pastry. Carefully remove remaining plastic.

4. Trim edge of the pastry with sharp knife; reserve scraps.

5. Spoon cold filling evenly into pastry case, brush edge of pastry with lightly beaten egg white.

6. Roll out remaining pastry as before, cover filling with pastry. Press edges together firmly, trim with knife. Using fingers, as shown, pinch edges to make a frill.

7. Roll reserved pastry scraps between sheets of plastic wrap, cut leaf shapes from pastry, if desired. Mark veins on leaves using small knife. Brush pastry with egg white, place leaves in position, brush leaves with egg white. Sprinkle pie evenly with extra sugar. Bake in moderately hot oven for 20 minutes, reduce heat to moderate, bake further 20 minutes or until pie is golden brown.

8. Lemony Apple Filling: Peel apples, cut into quarters, remove cores. Cut each quarter in half lengthways. Place apples into large saucepan with water, bring to boil, reduce heat, cover, cook for about 5 minutes or until apples are just tender. Transfer apples to bowl, gently stir in sugar, cinnamon and lemon rind; cool to room temperature.

BATTERS

A batter is made from a combination of flour and liquid. Batters can have a variety of other ingredients added to make pancakes, crêpes, waffles, pikelets, American hot cakes and many types of fritters. Batters are also used to coat and bind various foods together before frying. If you have time to allow a batter to stand, the results will be slightly better than if it is used as soon as it is made. The mixture will become slightly thicker and you will need to add a little more liquid; usually about 2 tablespoons to the quantities given in our recipes. Add this extra liquid a little at a time until mixture is easily pourable. Of course, this means you get another pancake in the batch!

PIKELETS

Pikelets are quick to make from basic ingredients and ideal if visitors drop in unexpectedly. There are many variations on the basic pikelet recipe. You can experiment with the flour. Substitute half wholemeal self-raising flour for half the white self-raising flour.

Finely chopped dried fruit can be added to the batter and, of course, spices such as cinnamon, ginger, nutmeg and mixed spice add interest. Plain pikelets are usually served with jam and butter or jam and cream.

BASIC PIKELETS

Pikelets are at their best served within several hours of being made. They can be frozen for up to 2 months; layer them on a flat tray with freezer wrap between them. This recipe is not suitable to microwave.

1 cup self-raising flour
¼ cup castor sugar
¼ teaspoon bicarbonate of soda
1 egg
¾ cup milk, approximately
1 teaspoon white vinegar
15g butter, melted

1. Sift flour, sugar and soda into medium bowl, make well in centre. Gradually stir in combined egg, milk and vinegar, stir until smooth. Stir in butter. Batter can be made in blender or processor; combine all ingredients, blend until smooth.

ABOVE: Basic Pikelets.

China board & pot: The Bay Tree; tiles: The Bay Tile Co.

2. Heat electric frying pan to 6½ or 175 degrees Celsius, or heat medium heavy-based frying pan over medium heat. Lightly grease pan evenly with butter. It should not be necessary to grease again; excess greasing will give you white spots on the first cooked side of the pikelets. Drop dessertspoons of batter into pan from

tip of spoon; this will make rounded pikelets. Allow room for spreading.
3. When bubbles start to appear, but just before they burst, turn pikelets with slide or spatula and cook until golden brown on the other side (this side will not take as long to cook as the first side). Do not turn pikelets back over onto the first side; this will only toughen them. If pikelets are cooked for too long on the first side, they will have a white rim around the edge.

Makes about 20.

PANCAKES

Pancakes are delicious eaten while they are hot, spread with a little butter and sprinkled with sugar and lemon or lime juice. The good thing about pancakes is that they are easy to make, can be frozen for future use, layered with freezer wrap between them, and can be used as a basis for sweet and savoury recipes.

An almost flat pan with a heavy base measuring about 20cm is ideal for cooking pancakes. Some cooks like to keep the pan for this use only. In this case, once it has been seasoned by use, there is no need to wash it; just wipe dry with a pad of absorbent paper. Keep the pan away from dust and other utensils which might scratch the surface.

If using an aluminium pan it should be "seasoned" by heating the pan then "polishing" it vigorously with some coarse cooking salt. A pad of absorbent paper makes an ideal "polisher". To season a copper pan, place a knob of butter into the pan, heat the pan until the butter burns. Use a pad of absorbent paper to wipe pan.

PANCAKES WITH LEMON AND SUGAR

If pancakes are to be eaten warm, they are at their best prepared just before serving. Pancakes can be frozen for up to 2 months. This recipe is not suitable to microwave.

1 cup plain flour
1 egg, lightly beaten
1 cup milk, approximately
butter
sugar
lemon or lime juice

1. Sift flour into medium bowl, make well in centre, gradually whisk or stir in egg and enough milk to make a thin, smooth batter. Alternatively, combine flour, egg and milk in blender or processor, blend or process until mixture is combined and smooth.

2. Heat heavy-based pan over high heat for a few minutes; pan should be very hot. Add about ½ teaspoon butter, swirl around pan until it is greased all over the base. Pour about

2 to 3 tablespoons batter from jug into centre of pan, quickly tilt pan so that batter runs from centre around edge.

3. When pancake is lightly browned underneath, turn and brown other side. This can be done with a spatula, egg slide or your fingers or pancake can be tossed and flipped over back into the pan; this takes a little practice.

ABOVE: Pancakes with Lemon and Sugar.

Plate: The Bay Tree; teapot & sugar container: The Australian East India Co.; tiles: The Bay Tile Co.

4. Serve pancakes as they are made onto warm plates; spread 1 side with a little butter, sprinkle with sugar and a little lemon or lime juice.

Makes about 10.

CUSTARDS

Custard is a combination of milk, eggs, sugar and flavouring. With these ingredients, you can make a stirred custard as sauce for desserts, or bake the mixture to form a set custard of many different types. Stirred custard is best cooked over simmering water (see Pineapple Upside-Down Cake) and a set custard is usually baked by placing the dish in a water bath or bain marie (see Crème Caramel recipe for how to do this); water protects the mixture from becoming too hot and curdling.

Eggs have amazing setting properties. One large fresh egg will thicken and set (depending on the cooking method) 1 cup milk. The more eggs added to milk (and/or cream) the firmer the custard will set. In this section, we show you how to make a glamorous crème caramel, a homely bread and butter custard and a rice custard. There is also a delicious trifle using packaged custard powder.

1. Whisk eggs, sugar, essence and milk together in medium bowl, add rice and sultanas.

2. Pour mixture into ovenproof dish (4 cup capacity), place dish into baking dish with enough boiling water to come half-way up sides of dish.

Bake in moderate oven for 35 minutes. Slip a fork underneath skin of custard, stir to distribute rice through custard evenly. Bake further 15 minutes; stir again with fork.

Sprinkle the custard with nutmeg or cinnamon, cook further 15 minutes or until just set.

Serves 4.

ABOVE: Baked Rice Custard.

Spoon and blue plate: The Bay Tree; tiles: Country Floors

RICE CUSTARD

Baking rice in custard was originally done to use up left-over rice. If you need to start from scratch, you will need to cook 2 tablespoons rice to get the ½ cup cooked rice required for this recipe (see glossary).

The gentle stirring of the rice through the custard during cooking will help distribute the rice evenly; this stops a layer of rice lying on the base of the dish. Any chopped dried fruit would be delicious in this dessert.

BAKED RICE CUSTARD

Custard will keep for up to a week in refrigerator; it will not reheat successfully. Recipe unsuitable to freeze or microwave.

3 eggs, lightly beaten
⅓ cup castor sugar
1 teaspoon vanilla essence
2½ cups milk
½ cup cooked rice
¼ cup sultanas
½ teaspoon ground nutmeg or
**   cinnamon**

BAKED CUSTARD

Bread and butter custard is an old English favourite originally devised to use up stale bread. The bread needs to be a little dry for best results; fresh bread will just be stodgy.

Use the jam and dried fruit of your choice. If the dried fruit is hard, soak the chopped fruit in a little boiling water for about 30 minutes or until it is soft; drain well before using.

BREAD AND BUTTER CUSTARD

Custard can be made about 4 days ahead; it is delicious served cold with cream or added fruit. It will not reheat successfully. Recipe unsuitable to freeze or microwave.

3 eggs
2 tablespoons castor sugar
1 teaspoon vanilla essence
2½ cups milk
30g butter
4 tablespoons apricot jam
8 slices stale white bread
½ cup chopped dried apricots
¼ teaspoon ground cinnamon
or nutmeg

1. Whisk eggs, sugar and essence together in a medium bowl, whisk in milk gradually.

2. Spread butter and jam on each slice of bread, trim away crusts; cut bread into halves or finger-length pieces. Place layer of bread into ovenproof dish (3 cup capacity). Add apricots, add half custard mixture, stand for 10 minutes to allow bread to soften.

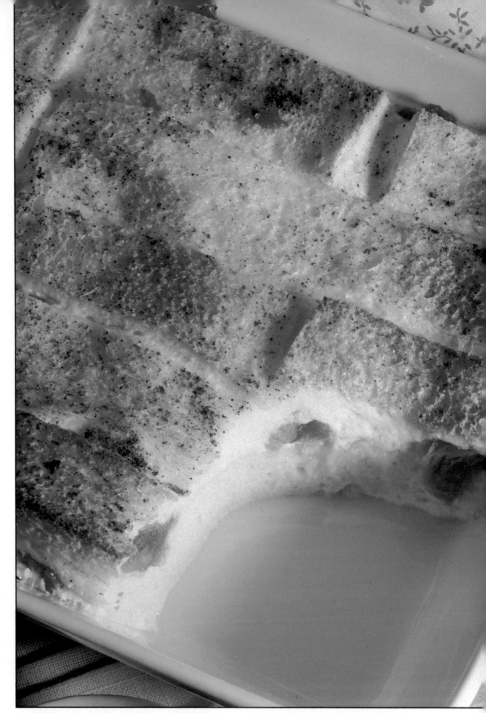

3. Place remaining bread, buttered-side-down, into dish; add remaining custard, sprinkle lightly with cinnamon or nutmeg.

ABOVE: Bread and Butter Custard.

4. Stand dish in baking dish, add enough boiling water to come halfway up sides of baking dish. Bake in moderate oven for about 40 minutes or until just set.
   Serves 4.

COOKING IN A WATER BATH

Cooking food in a water bath or bain marie is a method which prevents the temperature of the food from rising too much while it is in the oven. Crème Caramel (or caramel custard) is a perfect example. If this dessert were cooked without the water bath, it would probably reach boiling point and would curdle.

The caramel is simply burnt sugar; our method using water makes it easy to handle for beginner cooks. When you are more confident about sugar cookery, you can put the ¾ cup sugar into a pan and melt it over a fairly high heat until it turns golden brown. The caramel will taste the same; you will have simply omitted the step of boiling the water away.

Crème Caramel is a rich, classic dessert; it is spectacular in appearance and taste, yet is simple to make. It is important to add boiling water to the baking dish in which the pan of crème caramel is to be cooked.

When the dessert is cooked, it will still appear to be wobbly in the middle. If you are in doubt about whether the custard will set or not on cooling, insert the blade of an ordinary table knife into the centre of the custard, about halfway through.

If the knife has milk on the blade when you remove it, leave the custard in the oven for about another 5 minutes before testing again. If the knife is clean, then the custard is set.

Remember to remove the dessert from the water in the baking dish, or the custard will continue to cook and might curdle. It is important to allow the crème caramel to come to room temperature before refrigerating it overnight.

By refrigerating the dessert overnight, all the caramel will liquefy and will come out of the pan with the caramel to make the sauce. Be sure to choose a serving plate deep enough to contain it, or one with an edge or lip to catch the caramel.

CREME CARAMEL

Dessert is best prepared a day ahead; it will keep, covered, in refrigerator for up to 4 days. Recipe unsuitable to freeze or microwave.

¾ cup castor sugar
¾ cup water
6 eggs
2 teaspoons vanilla essence
⅓ cup castor sugar, extra
1¾ cups milk
300ml carton thickened cream

1. Combine sugar and water in medium heavy-based saucepan, stir constantly with wooden spoon over medium heat, without boiling, until sugar is dissolved. Use pastry brush dipped in water to brush any sugar crystals down from side of pan before mixture boils.

2. Bring sugar mixture to boil, boil rapidly, uncovered, without stirring, for about 5 minutes or until mixture turns light golden brown.

3. Pour caramel into deep 20cm round cake pan (it doesn't need greasing); hold pan with cloth. Quickly tilt pan to coat base evenly. There is no need to spread the caramel up side of pan. It is correct the caramel sets at this stage.

4. Lightly whisk eggs, essence and extra sugar together in bowl. Do not over-beat or custard will be too aerated. Combine milk and cream in saucepan, bring to boil, allow bubbles to subside from edge of pan. Gradually whisk milk mixture into egg mixture; strain into cake pan over caramel.

5. Place cake pan in baking dish with enough boiling water to come halfway up side of pan. Bake in moderately slow oven for about 40 minutes or until custard is just set; it will set more on cooling. Remove from water, stand several hours to cool to room temperature. Cover pan, refrigerate overnight. This method will ensure the caramel will coat the custard when it is turned out.

Use your fingers to pull the top of the custard from around the side of pan. It shouldn't stick to pan, but, if you're in doubt, run around the edge of the custard carefully with a knife or spatula. Invert custard onto serving dish, serve with whipped cream.

RIGHT: Crème Caramel.

Plate: Incorporated Agencies

1. Cut cake into even-sized pieces. Place into serving dish, sprinkle evenly with sweet sherry.

2. Combine jelly crystals with boiling water in medium bowl, stir until jelly is dissolved; stir in cold water. Transfer mixture to jug, gently pour jelly over back of spoon onto cake to prevent breaking cake. Refrigerate until set.

3. Custard: Place milk in medium saucepan, bring to boil. Blend custard powder and sugar with extra milk in small bowl, stir until smooth. Gradually stir into milk in the saucepan, stir constantly over medium heat until mixture boils and thickens; stir in sherry, cover, stand 10 minutes. Place peaches over jelly, top with custard, refrigerate until set. Whip cream and sifted icing sugar together until soft peaks form, use to decorate or spread over trifle; add extra fruit, if desired.

Serves 4.

SIMPLE EGGLESS CUSTARD

Trifle is always a winner for all age groups, and is a luscious way to dress up plain cake with jelly, custard, fruit and cream. You can vary the ingredients to suit yourself or what is on hand. We like the method of setting the cake in jelly as a base, but some people like to place the cake in the bowl, sprinkle it with orange juice or sherry, then add jelly and custard, nuts and fruit, according to the texture and flavour required.

The custard can be made over direct heat (not over water) because it contains custard powder and can withstand boiling. However, a custard using eggs as thickening should be made in a double saucepan (see Pineapple Upside-Down Cake).

TRIFLE

You can use bought or left-over sponge, butter cake or madeira cake for this recipe. Trifle can be made up to a week before required; keep, covered, in refrigerator. Recipe unsuitable to freeze or microwave.

150g cake
2 tablespoons sweet sherry
85g packet raspberry jelly crystals
1 cup boiling water
½ cup cold water
425g can sliced peaches, drained
½ cup thickened cream
2 teaspoons icing sugar
CUSTARD
1¾ cups milk
¼ cup custard powder
2 tablespoons castor sugar
¼ cup milk, extra
1 tablespoon sweet sherry

ABOVE LEFT: Trifle.

Bowl and serviette rings: Made Where; tea-towel: Opus; tiles: Pazotti

DESSERTS

There is a trend back to serving the good, old, tried and true desserts of yesteryear at dinner parties. In this section, there are two puddings that make their own sauces; ever-popular chocolate mousse, and an easy (but glamorous) cold soufflé. There is also old-fashioned upside-down cake and a fruit crumble, plus we tell you the secrets of mastering the perfect pavlova.

SELF-SAUCING DESSERT

Lemon Delicious is a magic dessert which makes its own sauce. The simple mixture separates into 2 layers during the cooking to give you a light, spongy top and a lemony sauce underneath. It can also be made in 4 dishes of about ¾ cup capacity each; cooking time for these 4 individual puddings will be about 25 minutes.

LIGHT 'N' LUSCIOUS LEMON DELICIOUS

Dessert must be made, then served immediately. This recipe is not suitable to freeze or microwave.

3 eggs
½ cup castor sugar
1 cup milk
1 tablespoon self-raising flour
½ cup lemon juice

1. Separate eggs; place whites and yolks into 2 separate small bowls (see glossary). Add sugar to egg yolks in small bowl, beat with electric mixer until thick and creamy. Gradually beat in milk on low speed, then sifted flour and lemon juice. Pour into large bowl.

ABOVE: Light 'n' Luscious Lemon Delicious.

Background: Abet Laminati

2. Beat egg whites in small bowl with electric mixer until soft peaks form (see glossary). Fold into egg yolk mixture in 2 batches. Use a plastic spatula for this; do not stir or beat or

you will deflate the mixture. Mixture will look a bit curdled, but this is correct.

3. Pour mixture into deep ovenproof dish (4 cup capacity). Stand dish in baking dish, add enough boiling water to baking dish to come halfway-up side of ovenproof dish. Bake in moderate oven for about 45 minutes or until firm to touch. Sprinkle with a little sifted icing sugar, if desired.
Serves 4.

CHOCOLATE SELF-SAUCING PUDDINGS

Puddings can be eaten cold, but are at their best eaten after making. Recipe is unsuitable to freeze or microwave.

1 cup self-raising flour
¾ cup castor sugar
¼ cup cocoa
½ cup milk
30g butter, melted
¾ cup brown sugar, firmly packed
¼ cup cocoa, extra
1¼ cups hot water

1. Sift flour, sugar and cocoa into medium bowl. Make well in centre, use wooden spoon to gradually stir in combined milk and butter, beat until smooth. Pour into 4 ovenproof dishes (¾ cup capacity).

2. Combine brown sugar and sifted extra cocoa in jug, gradually stir in hot water, stir until smooth. Gently pour the mixture evenly over the top of each pudding, place dishes onto an oven tray to make them easy to handle. Bake in moderate oven 35 minutes or until puddings have risen to the top of the dishes and are firm to touch. Dust with a little sifted icing sugar just before serving, if desired.

Serves 4.

SELF-SAUCING PUDDING

Under the chocolate pudding is a luscious sauce created by the simple addition of brown sugar, cocoa and hot water poured carefully over the mixture before baking.

Self-saucing puddings made individually put them into the "smart to serve at dinner parties" category. Serve them with ice-cream and/or whipped cream sweetened and flavoured with a tablespoon of your favourite liqueur.

ABOVE: Chocolate Self-Saucing Pudding.

Pyramid: Opus; tiles: Pazotti

If you want to make this pudding in a single dish, you will need a dish of 4 cup capacity, and it will take about 50 minutes to cook.

96

FRUIT CRUMBLE

This popular dessert is quick and easy. You can spread the crispy, crunchy topping over any drained, canned fruit of your choice instead of the apples in this recipe; any stewed fruit would be delicious as well.

And, instead of the mixed dried fruit, use any dried fruit you prefer. Chopped dates or apricots would be a pleasant change. Serve the crumble hot with custard, cream or ice-cream.

APPLE AND DRIED FRUIT CRUMBLE

We used Granny Smith apples in this recipe. Crumble can be prepared ready for cooking up to 2 days ahead; keep, covered, in refrigerator. Recipe unsuitable to freeze or microwave.

2 large apples
½ cup dried mixed fruit
1 tablespoon water
1 tablespoon lemon juice
¼ cup rolled oats
1 tablespoon coconut
2 tablespoons plain wholemeal flour
¼ teaspoon ground cinnamon
30g butter
¼ cup brown sugar

1. Peel, quarter, core and slice apples, combine in medium saucepan with fruit, water and juice. Bring to boil, reduce heat, cover, simmer for about 5 minutes or until apples are soft. Pour mixture into shallow ovenproof dish (3 cup capacity).

2. Combine oats, coconut, flour and cinnamon in small bowl, rub in butter with fingertips until mixture is coarse and crumbly. Stir in sugar.

3. Sprinkle mixture evenly over fruit mixture, bake in moderate oven for about 30 minutes or until topping is golden brown.

Serves 2.

MICROWAVE COOKING OF APPLES

Place sliced apples, fruit, water and juice in large shallow microwave-proof dish, cover, cook on HIGH for about 3 minutes or until apples are soft; proceed as above.

BELOW: Apple and Dried Fruit Crumble.

Shaker: The Australian East India Co., tea-towel: Opus; tiles: Pazotti

COLD SOUFFLES

A cold soufflé is not really a soufflé, but acquires this name because it is light and fluffy in texture. These berry soufflés are not difficult to make, but require gentle folding of the mixtures to prevent them from deflating.

You can double this recipe to make a soufflé in a large dish of 4 cup capacity to serve 4 people.

Any berries, fresh or frozen, can be used, or a combination of different types of berries is pleasant. However, we have used raspberries here as we like their colour and flavour.

BERRY CREAM SOUFFLES

Soufflés can be made up to 2 days ahead; keep, covered, in refrigerator. Recipe unsuitable to freeze.

100g frozen raspberries, thawed
1 tablespoon water
1 tablespoon gelatine
1 tablespoon water, extra
2 eggs, separated
2 tablespoons castor sugar
½ cup thickened cream
1 tablespoon castor sugar, extra
1 tablespoon coconut

1. Cut 2 strips greaseproof paper long enough to wrap around 2 soufflé dishes (¾ cup capacity) and to extend 3cm above edge of dishes. Secure joins with sticky tape.

2. Blend or process raspberries with water until smooth; strain. Sprinkle gelatine over extra water in small bowl, dissolve in hot water (or microwave on HIGH for about 20 seconds).

3. Combine egg yolks and sugar in medium bowl or top of double saucepan, stir constantly over simmering water (do not allow water to touch base of bowl or top saucepan) until mixture thickens slightly; stir in dissolved gelatine. Transfer to medium bowl, cool to room temperature; do not allow to set.

4. Whip cream until firm peaks form. Fold raspberry purée into egg yolk mixture, then whipped cream; use plastic spatula for this.

5. Place egg whites into small bowl, beat on high speed with electric mixer or rotary beater until soft peaks form. Gradually beat in extra sugar, beat until it is dissolved.

6. Fold egg white mixture gently and lightly into raspberry cream mixture, using plastic spatula.

7. Pour raspberry mixture into prepared dishes, level tops lightly with spatula, refrigerate several hours or until firm.

8. Gently remove paper collars from dishes; press coconut around sides of soufflés. Decorate with extra whipped cream and raspberries, if desired.
    Serves 2.

RIGHT: Berry Cream Soufflés.

Spoon and tea-towel: Australian East India Co., tiles: Country Floors

MERINGUE

A pavlova is simply a large meringue which is filled with cream and fruit. The pavlova should be dry and crisp on the outside and soft and marshmallowy on the inside.

Pavlovas cause more concern and trouble to cooks than most other desserts. If you can make a good pavlova consistently you will be dubbed an expert.

There are several factors which control the quality of the pavlova, and you will begin to understand why every pavlova is slightly different after reading this.

Cooks and scientists argue about the egg whites. Some say egg whites are best beaten at room temperature; others say to beat them at refrigerator temperature. We found eggs at both temperatures could be beaten satisfactorily to a good volume. When it is wet or humid you are unlikely to get good results for meringue making, due to the sugar content.

The whites should be super fresh and of good quality. Freshness is difficult to gauge unless you have your own egg-laying hens. Apparently, the diet of the hens and the time of the year can also affect the egg whites.

The best advice we can give you is to use large egg whites and be fanatical about dissolving every last grain of sugar.

Don't worry if the pavlova cracks in a few spots; the next time it could crack more or less; cover the cracks with cream!

MARSHMALLOW PAVLOVA

Pavlova can be made up to a day ahead; cover, keep at room temperature. Pavlova is best filled an hour before serving. Recipe unsuitable to freeze or microwave.

4 egg whites
1 cup castor sugar
1. Place egg whites in small bowl, beat with electric mixer on high speed for about 1 minute or until soft peaks form (see glossary). Gradually add sugar, a tablespoon at a time. Beat each addition of sugar until it is completely dissolved before adding the next spoonful. Scrape any sugar grains down from side of bowl and from

beaters several times. The beating process will take about 10 minutes, depending on room temperature, humidity and size of egg whites.
2. Lightly grease an oven tray. Sprinkle tray with a little plain flour, shake away excess flour. Mark 18cm circle on tray; use plate or cake pan for this.

3. Scrape all the meringue into the circle. Using spatula, carefully spread meringue to cover the circle on prepared tray, as shown. Try to make side of meringue as straight as possible. Make furrows up side, as shown. Furrows add stability to pavlova while it is cooking.

4. Level top of pavlova. Bake in very slow oven for 1 to 1½ hours or until it feels dry and crisp. Turn oven off, leave oven door ajar, cool pavlova in oven; this will take about an hour. Using sharp knife, carefully cut around top edge of the pavlova. Push crisp centre down gently so it rests on marshmallow in the middle; sometimes the centre will fall itself. This makes room for the filling and fruit of your choice.

RIGHT: Marshmallow Pavlova.

Plate: Incorporated Agencies

UPSIDE-DOWN CAKE

This type of cake looks very tempting when turned out, for you place the decoration in the pan before spreading with the cake mixture.

Serve cake hot or warm with custard or cream; it tends to dry out quickly when it becomes cold.

Any canned, well-drained fruit, such as apples, pears or peaches, can be used instead of the pineapple. Dates, walnuts or pecans are delicious additions to these fruits.

Stirred custard has no custard powder; it uses eggs for thickening.

PINEAPPLE UPSIDE-DOWN CAKE WITH STIRRED CUSTARD

This recipe is not suitable to freeze or microwave.

225g can sliced pineapple
60g butter
½ cup brown sugar
3 glacé cherries, halved
90g butter, extra
½ cup castor sugar
2 eggs
1½ cups self-raising flour
2 tablespoons milk
STIRRED CUSTARD
2 eggs
2 tablespoons castor sugar
1 teaspoon vanilla essence
1¼ cups milk

1. Drain pineapple, reserve 2 tablespoons syrup. Split pineapple slices in half horizontally to give 6 thin slices.

2. Grease 20cm ring pan. Beat butter and brown sugar in small bowl with electric mixer until just combined; do not over-beat. Spread mixture evenly over base of prepared pan.

3. Arrange the pineapple slices and cherries over brown sugar mixture.

4. Cream extra butter and sugar in small bowl with electric mixer until light and fluffy; add eggs 1 at a time, beat well after each addition. Stir in sifted flour, reserved pineapple syrup and milk in 2 batches.

5. Spread cake mixture evenly over pineapple and cherries. Bake in moderate oven for about 45 minutes or until skewer comes out clean when inserted into cake.

6. Stand cake 5 minutes. Place serving plate on top of cake pan, turn over carefully; lift pan away from cake.

7. Stirred Custard: Combine eggs, sugar and essence in top half of double saucepan or medium bowl that will fit inside top of a saucepan. Put water in base part of double saucepan or in saucepan under the bowl. Water should not touch base of top saucepan or bowl.

Bring water to boil, place top half of saucepan or bowl in position, reduce heat so the water is just simmering.

Heat milk in separate saucepan (or microwave oven on HIGH for about 1 minute) until milk is fairly warm. Stir milk into egg mixture, stir constantly over simmering water until mixture is slightly thickened. This could take up to 10 minutes, depending on heat of milk. Picture shows a test for correct consistency of custard.

Immediately custard has thickened, remove top of double saucepan or bowl from over the water. This is to stop the cooking process and prevent curdling. Custard will thicken a little more away from the heat.

Makes about 1½ cups.

RIGHT: Pineapple Upside-Down Cake with Stirred Custard.

Plates: Dansab; spoon: The Bay Tree

QUICK AND EASY MOUSSE

A mousse is a light, fluffy and luscious dessert which can contain cream, gelatine or egg whites, depending on the recipe. Chocolate mousse is one of the most popular.

You can double or triple this recipe to make 4 or 6 desserts. It is easy and quick to make. Allow 2 hours minimum setting time in the refrigerator. Serve chocolate mousse with extra whipped cream, if you like; it tends to tone down the richness of the chocolate.

Use a good-quality dark cooking chocolate for best results, and take care not to let water touch the chocolate or drop into it during the melting process (see glossary).

EASY RICH CHOCOLATE MOUSSE

Mousse can be prepared up to 3 days ahead; keep, covered, in refrigerator. Recipe unsuitable to freeze.

100g dark chocolate, chopped
1 egg, separated
½ cup thickened cream
2 teaspoons castor sugar

1. Place chocolate in medium bowl over saucepan of simmering water or in top half of double saucepan over simmering water; do not allow water to touch base of bowl or base of top saucepan. Heat gently (or microwave on HIGH for about 1 minute) until chocolate is melted. Transfer chocolate to medium bowl, quickly whisk in egg yolk and cream, whisk until smooth.

2. Place egg white in small bowl, beat with electric mixer or rotary beater until soft peaks form (see glossary); add sugar, beat until dissolved.

3. Gently fold egg white mixture into chocolate mixture with spatula. Pour mousse into glasses, refrigerate for several hours or until set; overnight is best. Serve topped with extra grated chocolate, if desired.
   Serves 2.

ABOVE LEFT: Easy Rich Chocolate Mousse.

Dessert glasses: The Australian East India Co., background: Abet Laminati

BAKING

Baking usually revolves around just a few ingredients; that is, butter, sugar, eggs and flour. The variations are countless; the additions and methods are what make them all so interesting to prepare.

MUFFINS

American-style muffins are even quicker, easier and less messy to make than scones. It is a one-bowl method of mixing. The butter is rubbed into the dry ingredients, then flavourings are lightly mixed in, then the egg and milk. The less mixing, the better; a fork is the ideal implement.

We used deep American-style muffin pans; these are a little over ⅓ cup capacity. The smaller variety hold about ¼ cup mixture. Muffins cooked in these smaller pans will take about 15 minutes to cook.

We have given you a basic muffin recipe with apricots, plus 2 variations, both simple to make. It is interesting to adapt these basic quantities of flour, butter and liquid to suit many different flavoured muffins.

Muffins are at their best freshly cooked and eaten warm with butter, but can be kept in an airtight container for up to 2 days. Muffins can be frozen for up to 2 months. Recipe unsuitable to microwave.

Clockwise from left: Basic Muffins with Apricots; Wholemeal Fig Muffins; Bacon and Fresh Herb Muffins.

Pan & rack: The Australian East India Co.

105

BASIC MUFFINS WITH APRICOTS

1 cup chopped dried apricots
3 cups self-raising flour
½ cup castor sugar
125g butter, chopped
½ cup milk
2 eggs, lightly beaten

1. Place apricots in small bowl, cover with boiling water, cover, stand 30 minutes, drain well.

2. Sift flour and sugar into large bowl, rub in butter with fingertips.

3. Add well-drained apricots to flour and butter mixture.

4. Combine milk and eggs in jug, mix with fork, add to flour mixture.

5. Mix with fork only until ingredients are combined; do not over-mix. Mixture should be coarse and lumpy.

6. Drop heaped tablespoons of mixture into well-greased deep, straight-sided muffin pans. Bake in moderately hot oven for about 20 minutes. Turn from pans onto wire racks to cool.

Makes about 12.

WHOLEMEAL FIG MUFFINS

2 cups wholemeal self-raising flour
1 cup white self-raising flour
½ cup raw sugar
125g butter, chopped
1 cup chopped dried figs
2 eggs, lightly beaten
1 cup milk

Sift flours and sugar into large bowl, rub in butter, add figs, then combined eggs·and milk. Proceed as for Basic Muffin recipe.

BACON AND FRESH HERB MUFFINS

6 bacon rashers
3 cups self-raising flour
60g butter
1 tablespoon chopped fresh basil
2 tablespoons chopped fresh chives
2 teaspoons chopped fresh oregano
¾ cup grated parmesan cheese
2 eggs, lightly beaten
1 cup milk

Chop bacon finely, place in small frying pan, cook over medium heat until crisp, drain on absorbent paper; cool. Sift flour into large bowl, rub in butter, add bacon, herbs and cheese, then combined eggs and milk. Proceed as for Basic Muffin recipe.

TEACAKE

Warm teacake wedges, split and served with butter, are delightful to eat. The cake has a light, spongy texture and is quite simple to make successfully; it is vital to cream the butter, sugar and egg until the mixture is light and fluffy.

CINNAMON TEACAKE

Cake is at its best eaten when freshly made, served with butter. It can be frozen for 2 months. This recipe is not suitable to microwave.

60g butter
1 teaspoon vanilla essence
½ cup castor sugar
1 egg
1 cup self-raising flour
⅓ cup milk
15g butter, melted, extra
1 tablespoon castor sugar, extra
½ teaspoon ground cinnamon

1. Grease a deep 20cm round cake pan or deep 20cm sandwich pan, cover base with greaseproof or baking paper. Grease greaseproof paper lightly; it is not necessary to grease baking paper.

ABOVE: Cinnamon Teacake.

China: Woodheath Pottery; cane background: Raw Straw

2. Place butter and essence in small bowl, beat on medium speed with electric mixer until light and creamy; butter should be as white as possible. Gradually beat in sugar, beat until soft and creamy. Add egg, beat until light and fluffy.

3. Stir in half the sifted flour and half the milk, stir gently with wooden spoon until combined. Add remaining sifted flour and milk, stir gently until combined, then beat until smooth, using wooden spoon. Spread mixture into prepared pan, bake in moderate oven for about 25 minutes or until cake is slightly shrunken from side of pan. Stand cake 2 minutes before turning cake onto wire rack.

4. Brush cake with extra melted butter, sprinkle evenly with combined extra sugar and cinnamon.

SCONES

Scones served hot from the oven with butter or jam and cream are delightful for morning or afternoon tea. Often, cooks are judged by the scones they can make. There is no mystery about making light, fluffy scones; you must make a soft, sticky dough and the dough should be kneaded quickly and lightly. The rest is up to the oven; it should be very hot to make the scones rise quickly.

INGREDIENTS

Flour: If you like the taste and texture of wholemeal, try using half white self-raising flour and half wholemeal self-raising flour instead of all white flour; you will need a little more liquid to make the dough soft and sticky.

The amount of liquid needed to achieve a soft, sticky dough depends on the way the flour absorbs the liquid; this depends on the quality and the age of the flour.

Sugar: A little sugar added to a scone dough takes away the floury taste; you can use any type of sugar you like: raw, brown, white or icing sugar.

Liquid: The liquid added to scones can be varied. You can use cream or any type of milk, including buttermilk, which is fresh or has turned sour in the refrigerator.

Commercial sour cream or light sour cream or plain yoghurt can be used, too, but will need to be broken down with some water to make it a similar consistency to milk. Water can be used by itself, giving you a very pale scone. Water and milk or any other of the above-mentioned dairy products can be mixed together for the liquid.

Butter: Butter is an optional extra in scones; it adds a little flavour and colour to the cooked scones.

Salt: We haven't added salt to our recipe, but, if you like, a pinch of salt can be sifted with the flour.

HANDLING THE DOUGH

Scone dough should be patted out flat with your hand. A rolling pin is useful if making large quantities of dough. Don't roll dough heavily or too thinly.

CUTTERS

We like to use sharp metal cutters for scones; they don't squash the dough, but simply cut through it.

COOKING TIPS

We like to cook scones in a cake pan with side about 3cm or 4cm high. This gives the scones a "wall" to stop them toppling over, and it also allows them to brown evenly on top.

Don't squash scones into the pan; they should be just touching. They do expand as well as rise, and over-crowding will make it difficult to cook the scones in the middle.

It is vital to cook scones at a very high temperature. You do need to experiment with your oven to find the shelf position and the temperature that gives you the results you like the best.

As a guide, the hottest part of the oven will give you the best results for scones. This varies depending on the type of oven, the way the heat is distributed and the type of fuel used by the oven. Always check the oven manufacturer's instructions.

The scones in the middle of the pan will take the longest to cook. After the cooking time has expired, tap the centre scones firmly with fingertips; scones should sound hollow and look evenly browned.

Turn the scones onto a wire rack. If you want the scones to be soft, wrap them immediately in a clean tea-towel or table napkin. If you prefer the tops a little crisp, leave them on the rack to cool, uncovered.

BASIC SCONES

Scones are at their best eaten the day they are made. They can be frozen for 2 months. This recipe is not suitable to microwave.

2 cups self-raising flour
2 teaspoons sugar
15g butter, chopped
1 cup milk, approximately

1. Sift flour and sugar into medium bowl; rub in butter with fingertips.

2. Make well in centre of ingredients, add almost all the milk at once.

3. Using a knife, "cut" the milk through the flour mixture to mix to a soft, sticky dough. Add remaining milk only if needed for correct consistency.

4. Turn dough from bowl onto lightly floured surface.

5. Knead lightly until smooth.

6. Press dough out gently and evenly to approximately 2cm thickness. Don't use too much flour on the board or the balance of ingredients will be upset.

7. Dip 5cm cutter into flour, cut as many rounds as you can from the piece of dough. Place scones side by side, just touching, in lightly greased 20cm sandwich pan.

Gently knead dough into round shape again; the scones from the second handling will not be quite as

ABOVE: Basic Scones.

China: Appley Hoare Antiques; cloth & table: Chelsea House Antiques

light as those from the first. When patting the dough out, leave it a little thicker than the first time.

8. Brush tops with a little extra milk.

9. Bake in a very hot oven for about 15 minutes, or until tops are browned and scones sound hollow when tapped with fingertips.

Makes about 10.

BUTTER CAKE

We have given you a basic butter cake recipe and 3 simple variations. The butter cake is one of the most versatile of mixtures; it can be adapted to many flavours and textures.

BASIC BUTTER CAKE

Cake will keep for 2 days in airtight container. Cake can be frozen for up to 2 months. This recipe is not suitable to microwave.

125g butter
1 teaspoon vanilla essence
¾ cup castor sugar
2 eggs
1½ cups self-raising flour
½ cup milk

1. This first step can be done by hand with a wooden spoon, or, like us, using an electric mixer. Rinse bowl and beaters under hot water before mixing and dry well; this makes the process of creaming quicker.

Beat butter first with any flavouring that is included in the recipe, such as rinds or essences. The butter will absorb and develop the flavour. Butter should be beaten until it is as light in colour as possible.

Add sugar, beat just until mixture is light and fluffy in appearance; sugar should not be completely dissolved.

Add unbeaten eggs one at a time. Beat each egg into the mixture before adding the next egg. If eggs are added too quickly (or if they are cold from the refrigerator), the mixture will curdle. This will happen if eggs are too large.

2. If using a small bowl, remove bowl from mixer, transfer mixture to larger bowl for easier combining of ingredients. Add any fruit or nuts, mix lightly with wooden spoon.

Add about half the sifted dry ingredients, then half the liquid; mix ingredients together lightly with wooden spoon, do not beat. Add remaining dry ingredients and liquid, mix lightly. Mixture will look coarse in

texture. Now give a quick beating to make texture smoother and finer. Spread mixture into prepared pan and bake; see Cake Baking Tips, page 113.

FROSTED CHOCOLATE APRICOT RING

We cooked this cake in a 20cm ring pan. Cake will keep for 2 days in an airtight container. Uniced cake can be frozen for up to 2 months. Recipe unsuitable to microwave.

125g butter
1 teaspoon vanilla essence
¾ cup castor sugar
2 eggs
1⅓ cups self-raising flour
½ cup milk
¼ cup cocoa
⅓ cup Choc Bits
½ cup chopped glacé apricots
CHOCOLATE FROSTING
60g butter
1 cup icing sugar
1 tablespoon cocoa
1 tablespoon milk

Prepare as for basic butter cake but sift cocoa with the flour. Stir Choc Bits and apricots into mixture. Bake in moderate oven for about 45 minutes.
Chocolate Frosting: Beat butter in small bowl with electric mixer until creamy, gradually add sifted icing sugar and cocoa, then milk; beat until spreadable. Spread over cold cake.

PUMPKIN AND GINGER LOAF

You will need to cook about 300g pumpkin for this recipe. We used a 15cm x 25cm loaf pan. Cake will keep for 3 days in airtight container. Recipe unsuitable to microwave.

125g butter
1 teaspoon vanilla essence
¾ cup castor sugar
2 eggs
1½ cups self-raising flour
½ cup milk
2 teaspoons mixed spice
2 teaspoons ground ginger
⅓ cup chopped glacé ginger
1 cup cold mashed pumpkin
½ cup slivered almonds

LEFT: Clockwise from left: Pumpkin and Ginger Loaf; Frosted Chocolate Apricot Ring; Coconut Lime Streusel Cake.

China: Mikasa; rug: Australian East India Co.

Prepare as for basic butter cake, but add spices, ginger and pumpkin to cake mixture after the flour and milk have been added. Pour cake mixture into prepared pan, sprinkle evenly with almonds, bake in moderate oven for about 1 hour. Stand cake for 10 minutes before turning onto wire rack to cool.

COCONUT LIME STREUSEL CAKE

We used a deep 20cm round cake pan for this recipe. Cake will keep for 2 days in airtight container. Recipe unsuitable to microwave.

1 cup coconut
⅓ cup brown sugar
2 teaspoons grated lime rind
125g butter
1 teaspoon vanilla essence
¾ cup castor sugar

2 eggs
1½ cups self-raising flour
½ cup milk
1. Grease cake pan thickly with butter. Place coconut in heavy-based saucepan, stir constantly over medium heat until coconut is lightly browned. Transfer to bowl; cool to room temperature. Stir in brown sugar and lime rind. Sprinkle inside of prepared pan with coconut mixture, shake excess mixture back into bowl; reserve excess mixture for later.

2. Prepare cake as for basic butter cake. Spread half the cake mixture into prepared pan, sprinkle evenly with reserved coconut mixture. Using skewer, swirl coconut mixture through cake mixture, then top with remaining cake mixture. Bake in moderate oven for about 55 minutes. Stand cake for 5 minutes before turning onto wire rack to cool. Serve upside-down, warm or cold with whipped cream, if desired.

CAKE BAKING TIPS

INGREDIENTS

Butter and other shortenings: Butter will result in a cake which will keep better than a cake made from margarine. Cooking margarines and polyunsaturated margarines can be used in cake recipes, or a combination of these with butter. Best results will be obtained by having butter at room temperature; never melted.

Sugar: Castor sugar will give a finer textured cake than those made with ordinary white crystal sugar. Brown sugar and raw sugar should not be substituted for white sugar; the results will be different. Honey cannot be substituted for sugar; again, results will be different. Follow specific recipes. If sugar is lumpy, sift to remove lumps.

Eggs: All our recipes use 61g eggs; have them at room temperature for best results.

Flour: Use whichever flour is specified in recipe; do not substitute wholemeal flour for white flour; results and liquid content will be different. Fresh flour will absorb less liquid than older flour; this is why each time you make a cake the mixture could look slightly different. Experience will teach you when it is necessary to leave out or add a little more liquid than the recipe states.

OVEN POSITIONS AND TEMPERATURES

Ovens vary; always check maker's instructions for best results. As a general guide, the best position for cakes can be determined by placing the empty cake pan in the cold oven and estimating where the top of the cooked cake will be; the top of the cooked cake should be in the centre of the oven; adjust shelves accordingly. The only exception to this is when 2 shelves are being used.

If more than 1 cake is cooked at a time, provided they require the same temperature, they can be placed on the same shelf, either side by side or diagonally in the oven. However, the pans must not touch each other, the sides or back of the oven, or the door when it is closed.

If in doubt, check by placing the unfilled cake pans on the shelf before turning the oven on.

After half the cooking time has expired, reverse the positions of the pans, for even baking. If this is done fairly quickly, it will not hurt the cakes.

If using 2 shelves, position them so that there is clearance between the top of the pans on the lower shelf and the bottom of the top shelf; remember to allow room for cakes to rise.

Fan forced and convection ovens usually cook and brown evenly without the pans being swapped around.

Most cakes are cooked at a moderate temperature; check manufacturer's directions.

CAKE PANS

We like to use aluminium cake pans. Anodised pans, or those which have been coated with a non-stick surface, and cake pans which are made from tin or stainless steel will give satisfactory results if the oven temperature is reduced by 10 degrees Celsius (25 degrees Fahrenheit).

We use melted butter and a brush to grease cake pans evenly; it is a precaution to cover base of pan with greaseproof or baking paper to prevent cake sticking. Grease the greaseproof paper in the pan; it is not necessary to grease baking paper.

TO TEST IF A CAKE IS COOKED

Test cake just before cooking time has expired. Touch top of the cake with fingers; if firm, test with a skewer in the thickest part of the cake. If the skewer comes out free from any cake mixture, remove cake from oven. If cake mixture appears on skewer, test after further 5 minutes. Shake pan gently to make sure the cake is free from the pan. Turn onto wire rack. Then, so that rack does not mark the top of the cake, invert onto wire rack to finish cooling.

BASIC BUTTER CAKE SIZES AND COOKING TIMES

The basic butter cake mixture can be cooked in any of the following sized pans and will take approximately the time given below.

Deep 20cm round or 19cm square cake pan — 55 minutes.
14cm x 21cm and 15cm x 25cm loaf pans — 50 minutes.
20cm baba or ring pan — 35 minutes.
2 x 8cm x 26cm bar pans — 30 minutes.
19cm x 29cm lamington pans — 30 minutes.
2 x 18cm sandwich pans — 25 minutes.

ROCK CAKES

Rock cakes are quick to mix and make great portable food. They are ideal for picnics and lunch boxes and will take some rough treatment in a school bag! As an afternoon tea treat, try serving them hot from the oven with butter; they are delicious.

You can use half wholemeal self-raising flour, if you like, instead of all white self-raising flour, but you will need to add a little more milk to get the correct consistency.

Take care to get the consistency just right; the mixture should hold its shape when placed onto the tray; the cakes should spread only a little during the cooking time.

Use brown, raw or the coarser crystal sugar instead of castor sugar, if preferred. Change the fruit to whatever you like; currants, chopped dates, raisins and dried apricots are all good, as is the basic dried mixed fruit.

The uncooked rock cakes can be sprinkled with coarse raw sugar or crystal sugar for added sparkle.

BASIC ROCK CAKES

Cakes can be prepared up to 3 days ahead; keep in an airtight container. They can be frozen for 2 months. Recipe unsuitable to microwave.

2 cups self-raising flour
¼ teaspoon ground cinnamon
⅓ cup castor sugar
90g butter, chopped
1 cup sultanas
2 tablespoons mixed peel
1 egg, lightly beaten
⅓ cup milk, approximately

1. Sift flour, cinnamon and sugar into medium bowl, add butter, rub in with fingertips. Stir in fruit and peel with wooden spoon.

2. Make well in centre of dry ingredients, add egg, then enough milk to give a moist but still firm consistency. If mixture is too soft, cakes will spread too much during the cooking time.

ABOVE: Basic Rock Cakes.

Basket: Clay Things

3. Place 2 heaped tablespoons mixture onto lightly greased oven trays. Leave about 5cm between each cake to allow them to spread slightly.

4. Sprinkle cakes with a little extra sugar, if desired. Bake in moderately hot oven for about 15 minutes or until lightly browned. Use metal spatula to loosen cakes on trays; cool on trays.

Makes about 15.

SPONGE CAKE

Sponge cakes are easy to make; they require a light folding action (see glossary) and a good basic recipe such as this one. With the addition of a simple mock cream and glacé icing, you have a cake that looks professional enough to show off at any special occasion.

BIRTHDAY SPONGE

It is correct that there is no liquid in this sponge recipe. This icing will always crack as soon as it is cut. Sponge is best made the day it is required as there isn't any butter in the recipe to keep it moist. Unfilled sponge can be frozen for up to 2 months. Recipe unsuitable to microwave.

SPONGE
4 eggs
¾ cup castor sugar
⅓ cup plain flour
⅓ cup self-raising flour
⅓ cup cornflour
2 tablespoons strawberry jam
MOCK CREAM
⅓ cup water
½ cup sugar
125g butter
½ teaspoon vanilla essence
½ cup coconut
GLACE ICING
¾ cup icing sugar
½ teaspoon butter
2 teaspoons water, approximately orange colouring

1. Grease 2 deep 20cm or sandwich pans, line bases with paper, grease paper. Beat eggs in large bowl with electric mixer until thick and creamy, gradually add sugar, beat after each addition until sugar is dissolved. This will take about 10 minutes. It is important to dissolve the sugar; test a little of the mixture by rubbing between your thumb and forefinger to detect sugar grains.

2. Sift flours together 3 times to aerate and mix the flours evenly. Sift the flours over the egg mixture; use plastic spatula to fold the flours through the egg mixture. Use an upward and over action to mix well.

3. Pour mixture evenly into prepared pans, bake in moderate oven for about 20 minutes or until cakes are lightly browned and have shrunk slightly away from sides of pans. Turn onto wire racks immediately to cool. While cakes are cooking, prepare mock cream and toast coconut (see glossary).

4. Mock Cream: Combine water and sugar in small saucepan, stir constantly over high heat, without boiling, until sugar is dissolved, increase heat, bring to boil. Remove from heat, cool to room temperature. Beat butter and essence in small bowl with electric mixer until as white as possible. Gradually pour in syrup in a thin stream, while beating until light and fluffy.

5. When sponges are cold, place half onto serving plate, spread with jam and about ⅓ cup mock cream. Top with remaining sponge, reserve ⅓ cup mock cream for decorating sponge.

Spread remaining mock cream evenly around outside of cake. Place toasted coconut on sheet of greaseproof paper, roll sides of cake evenly in coconut, as shown.

6. Place reserved mock cream into piping bag fitted with fluted tube.

ABOVE: Birthday Sponge.

Plate & cloth: Appley Hoare Antiques

---

7. Gently squeeze piping bag, supporting with other hand, and pipe stars around top edge of cake.

8. Glacé Icing: Sift icing sugar into small heatproof bowl, stir in butter and enough water to give a stiff paste. Place bowl over saucepan of simmering water, stir constantly until icing is just warm and runny; do not over-heat or icing will crystallise. Tint icing with a little colouring.

9. Pour icing over cake, using spatula to quickly spread icing out to the mock cream edge. Allow icing to set for a few minutes before decorating.

CUITS

three biscuits we give you are ...ple, well-known favourites. Here are valuable points to help you become an expert biscuit maker:
- If butter has to be creamed (see glossary), have it at room temperature.
- Don't over-stir any biscuit mixture.
- Use flat oven trays or those with a tiny side for baking. You can also turn a flat cake pan or baking dish upside down and use the base for baking.
- Grease trays lightly and only where the biscuits are placed. There is no point in greasing the corners because the biscuits can't fit there and it only makes washing up difficult.
- Be careful not to over-cook biscuits; they will become crisp when they're cold. They should feel firm but soft when cooked. Give one biscuit a gentle push with a finger; a cooked biscuit will move on the tray, an uncooked one won't. Usually, the biscuits around the outside edge of the tray will be cooked first.
- Don't be afraid to open the oven during cooking and alternate the positions of trays. This helps the biscuits to brown evenly. Also, turn the trays. Some ovens tend to cook too quickly towards the back of the oven.
- Biscuits are usually cooked in the top half of the oven, but follow the oven maker's directions.
- Cool biscuits on trays or racks, as directed in individual recipes.

ANZAC BISCUITS

Make these as large or as small as you like. Biscuits will keep in airtight containers for at least a week or will freeze for 2 months. Recipe unsuitable to microwave.

1 cup rolled oats
1 cup plain flour
1 cup brown sugar, firmly packed
½ cup coconut
125g butter
2 tablespoons golden syrup
1 tablespoon water
½ teaspoon bicarbonate of soda
1. Combine oats, sifted flour, sugar and coconut in large bowl. Combine

butter, golden syrup and water in small saucepan, stir constantly over medium heat until butter is melted; stir in soda (or combine butter, golden syrup and water in microwave-proof jug, cook on HIGH for about 1 minute or until butter is melted). Stir in soda. Stir mixture into dry ingredients.
2. Place rounded teaspoons of mixture 5cm apart onto lightly greased oven trays; bake in moderately slow oven for about 20 minutes or until biscuits feel slightly firm. Use spatula to loosen biscuits on trays, cool on trays.
Makes about 25.

CORNFLAKE SULTANA COOKIES

Cookies will keep for at least a week in airtight container. Recipe unsuitable to freeze or microwave.

5 cups uncrushed cornflakes
1 cup coconut
½ cup brown sugar
1 cup sultanas
1 cup self-raising flour
185g butter, melted
2 eggs, lightly beaten
1. Combine cornflakes, coconut, sugar, sultanas and sifted flour in large bowl. Stir in butter and eggs gently with wooden spoon.

2. Shape rounded tablespoons of mixture into balls. Place about 5cm apart on greased oven trays. Bake in moderate oven for about 10 minutes or until lightly browned. Stand cookies for 3 minutes before lifting onto wire rack to cool.
Makes about 25.

MELTING MOMENTS

Unfilled biscuits can be kept for up to 2 weeks in an airtight container. Recipe unsuitable to freeze or microwave.

250g butter
⅓ cup icing sugar
1½ cups plain flour
½ cup cornflour
LEMON CREAM
60g butter
1 teaspoon grated lemon rind
½ cup icing sugar
3 teaspoons lemon juice
1. Have butter at room temperature. Combine butter and sifted icing sugar in small bowl, beat with electric mixer until light and fluffy. Stir in combined sifted flours in 2 batches.

2. Place mixture into large piping bag fitted with fluted tube. Pipe mixture in swirls about 3cm apart on lightly greased oven trays. Bake in moderate oven for about 10 minutes or until lightly browned. Stand few minutes, lift onto wire rack to cool. Join biscuits together with lemon cream.
3. Lemon Cream: Combine butter, rind and sifted icing sugar in small bowl, beat until light and fluffy; beat in juice.
Makes about 18.

RIGHT: From top: Anzac Biscuits; Melting Moments; Cornflake Sultana Cookies.

Boxes: The Australian East India Co.

EASY BAKED SLICE

This is an all-time favourite recipe with its delicious layers of a simple pastry base, jam and coconut topping. You can change the jam to whatever you happen to have in the cupboard; even marmalade is yummy!

RASPBERRY COCONUT SLICE

Slice can be prepared up to 2 days ahead; keep, covered, in refrigerator. It can be frozen for up to 2 months. Recipe unsuitable to microwave.

1½ cups plain flour
100g butter
1 egg yolk
2 tablespoons water, approximately
½ cup raspberry jam
2 cups coconut
2 eggs, lightly beaten
½ cup castor sugar

ABOVE: Raspberry Coconut Slice.

Tiles: Pazotti

1. Sift flour into medium bowl, rub in butter with fingertips. Add egg yolk to flour mixture, add enough water until you can press ingredients together with hand to make a firm dough.

2. Turn dough onto lightly floured surface, knead gently until smooth. Place dough into 19cm x 29cm lamington pan. Use flat-sided glass to roll dough evenly over base of pan (or use fingertips). Bake in moderately hot oven for about 20 minutes or until lightly browned; stand 10 minutes.

3. Spread jam evenly over pastry base.

4. Combine coconut, eggs and sugar in medium bowl, mix with fork until all the coconut is moist.

5. Spread coconut mixture evenly over jam; do not flatten mixture. Bake in moderate oven for about 20 minutes or until golden brown; cool in pan.

UNBAKED SLICE

This rich, delicious slice needs no baking, but sets quite quickly in the refrigerator. It is ideal for afternoon tea, as an after-dinner nibble for fêtes and 'take a plate' occasions.

CHOCOLATE SLICE

We used Marie biscuits in this recipe. Slice can be made up to a week ahead; keep, covered, in refrigerator. Recipe unsuitable to freeze.

200g packet white marshmallows
1 tablespoon water
90g unsalted butter
200g dark chocolate, chopped
125g plain sweet biscuits, roughly
 chopped
½ cup halved glacé cherries
½ cup roasted hazelnuts
½ cup pecans or walnuts
200g dark chocolate, extra
60g unsalted butter, extra

1. Combine marshmallows, water and butter in large saucepan. Stir constantly over low heat until marshmallows are melted.

2. Remove pan from heat, add chocolate, stir until melted.

3. Add biscuits, cherries and nuts to marshmallow mixture, stir gently until ingredients are combined.

4. Line 2 bar pans (8cm x 26cm) with strips of foil large enough to extend over long sides of pan to make slice easy to remove. Spread mixture evenly into prepared pans; do not crush biscuits. Refrigerate for 1 hour.

Melt extra chocolate and extra butter in bowl or double saucepan over saucepan of simmering water; water must not touch base of bowl or saucepan (see glossary). Spread mixture evenly over slices, refrigerate for 1 hour or until firm. Remove slices from pans, peel away foil.

BELOW: Chocolate Slice.

Plate: Village Living

GLOSSARY

TO PEEL TOMATOES

1. Cut small cross in base of each tomato.

2. Remove stem ends. Drop tomatoes into saucepan of boiling water, boil for 30 seconds. Place into bowl of iced water for 30 seconds before peeling.

TO REMOVE TOMATO SEEDS

Cut tomato in half, squeeze out seeds if tomato is fairly ripe and soft.

If tomato is firm, scrape seeds out carefully with teaspoon.

DRIED PEAS, BEANS AND LENTILS

Cover dried beans and peas well with water, stand overnight. Next day, drain then boil in plenty of water until beans are tender; time depends on type of bean used, this is somewhere between 30 minutes and an hour.

Lentils do not require soaking; they are boiled for about 15 minutes or until tender.

GREEN SHALLOTS

Used as an ingredient and a garnish. Pull off outside layer, trim root end. Cut away most of the dark green part as it tends to be a little slimy. Picture shows shallots prepared for various purposes.

Top row, from left: trimmed ready for chopping; cut into straws; cut into bonbons. For bonbons, cut length of shallot required, push a pin right through shallot about 1cm from end and draw pin carefully to end. Repeat several times at each end; drop into iced water to curl.

Second row, from left: chopped shallots, shallot straws curled by placing in iced water, and shallots sliced diagonally.

ASPARAGUS

1. Use vegetable peeler to scrape away large nodules from stem, leave the small nodules intact near tip.

2. Bend each spear of asparagus near the coarse end. You will feel a spot where spear will snap. Break away coarse end and discard it.

GARLIC

Use a garlic crusher for odour-free fingers. Place unpeeled clove (broken away from the knob) in bowl of crusher, press down with top half of crusher, discard peel and fibres remaining in bowl of crusher.

Another way to crush garlic: peel a clove, slice or chop on board with a pinch of salt. Using broad part of the knife blade, mash garlic by pushing the knife away from you.

AVOCADOS

1. Using sharp knife, cut all the way around the avocado. Twist into 2 pieces. Hold the half with the stone in one hand, hit stone sharply with blade of knife, twist knife to release stone.

2. Peel skin away, using fingers.

3. Avocado fan: Using sharp knife, cut in slices nearly to narrow end of avocado; fan slices as shown.

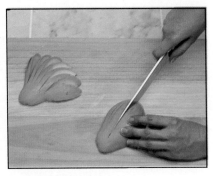

JULIENNE VEGETABLES

These are thin strips of almost any vegetable; cut strips as evenly as possible, for example, cut carrot as shown.

TO CHOP ONIONS

This method stops onions falling to pieces and being unmanageable during chopping. Some say to put unpeeled onions in refrigerator for an hour before chopping to prevent fumes from making you cry.

Peel onion by removing tough outer layers. Trim root end but leave root intact to help hold onion together during the chopping process.

1. Chopping: Cut onion in half lengthways. Place half, cut side down, on board. Hold onion as shown, cut lengthways as finely as possible.

2. Cut onion horizontally as far through to the root as possible. If onion is large, 2 or 3 cuts are necessary.

3. Hold onion as shown, cut across to chop as finely as required.

Slicing: Picture shows half onion being sliced and onions cut into wedges.

TO SEGMENT AN ORANGE

Cut peel away from orange, removing all white pith. Cut down to centre of orange between membranes joining segments.

TO CHOP PARSLEY

Place washed and dried sprigs on board. Using sharp knife, hold tip down with fingers and "rock" knife over parsley. You will gradually become very quick at this; it can be applied to many chopping needs.

CHOPPING CHINESE-STYLE

Most vegetables are chopped diagonally across the grain for Chinese-style cooking; onions are usually cut into wedges unless otherwise specified.

EQUIPMENT

As you progress with cooking techniques, you gradually acquire knives and equipment. It is not necessary to buy a complete set of saucepans; instead, we like to buy a saucepan that best suits a particular purpose.

We use sets of graduated measuring cups and spoons for measuring ingredients. Shake dry ingredients loosely into the cup required; do not pack firmly unless otherwise directed. Level top of cup or spoon with spatula or knife.

Always measure liquid with jug on flat surface; check at eye level for accuracy.

THERMOMETER

A candy thermometer (also used for gauging the heat of oil) is a worthwhile investment if you intend using it fairly often. It takes the guesswork out of making sweets. This is the correct way to use the thermometer. When not in use, store it in a safe place to avoid damage.

Never plunge the thermometer into boiling syrup without this preparation or it will probably break.

Place thermometer in saucepan of cold water, bring water to boil. Check that thermometer registers accurately on boiling point (100 degrees Celsius or 212 degrees Fahrenheit), make allowances for any inaccuracies when gauging the syrup. It is best to do this test each time you use the thermometer.

When syrup or oil reaches required temperature, remove thermometer, return to pan of boiling water, remove from heat, cool to room temperature in the water.

COOKING VEGETABLES

Most vegetables can be cooked by the methods of microwaving, steaming and boiling. Cooking in a microwave oven and steaming are the best methods in terms of speed and retention of colour, vitamins and minerals.

Microwave cooking: There are many different theories and opinions on how to cook individual vegetables for best results. Manufacturer's instructions and cookbooks specialising in microwave cookery will give you the best directions. Try all the different methods and decide the one you like the best.

Steaming: We used a stainless steel steamer (available from supermarkets and kitchen stores). This fits easily into medium to large saucepans, depending on how far the steamer is opened out. Make sure the saucepan has tight-fitting lid. There should be enough water to almost touch the base of the steamer; have water simmering the whole time the vegetables are being cooked. It is important to keep saucepan covered tightly during cooking.

Boiling: Vegetables should be barely covered with water. As a general rule, bring the vegetables to the boil, covered, reduce heat to keep the water simmering and cook until the vegetables are just tender. To cover or not to cover has always been controversial. The old-fashioned guideline was that if the vegetable grew in the dark (underground) then cook it in the dark, that is, with the lid on during the cooking time.

TO TEST IF STEAK IS COOKED

It can be difficult to determine the stage at which steak is ready to be served; experience is the best teacher. Picture shows, from left to right: fillet steak well done; medium rare; and rare.

Steak cooked to the rare stage is quite spongy and soft to the touch, as shown. Medium rare is less spongy and so on.

TO SEPARATE EGGS

A recipe may specify yolks and whites used separately. Crack shell by tapping gently on a flat surface or sharp edge, preferably not the mixing bowl, break shell in half and "see-saw" yolk between shells to allow white to run into bowl.

It is a safe idea to break each egg separately into a cup to ensure freshness before adding to other eggs.

If a recipe requires egg white to be beaten to a fluffy stage, it is vital that not a speck of yolk goes into the white or the white simply won't beat up. However, should this happen, use an eggshell half to remove the yolk from the white.

TO BEAT EGG WHITES

Egg whites are often beaten to "soft peaks" or "firm peaks". A little care is needed because if whites are over-beaten it makes them difficult to fold through another, usually heavier, mixture.

Soft peaks: This state of soft peaks shows round mounds of mixture after a short time of beating at a high speed.

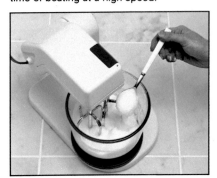

Firm peaks: Firm peaks are a slightly dryer, more peaked shape than the soft peak stage.

TO RUB IN BUTTER
Use fingertips and thumbs to rub butter through dry ingredients.

CREAMING
Add essence or any flavouring to chopped butter, beat in small bowl until mixture is as white as possible. Add sugar, beat until light and fluffy. You can also use your hand or a wooden spoon. Proceed as directed in individual recipes.

FOLDING IN
This method of mixing is important to master; the object is to combine the ingredients as evenly, gently and quickly as possible to prevent the light mixture from deflating.

We like to use a plastic spatula so ingredients can be easily incorporated from the base of the bowl through to the top surface of the mixture.

Once you've achieved this folding over and over action, you won't have any trouble making sponges, soufflés or mousses, etc.

BLENDING
This is the process of gradually stirring a liquid into a dry ingredient until the mixture is smooth (without lumps) and combined. Picture shows you how to blend cornflour and water together.

TO PUREE
Fruit, vegetables, meat, chicken, fish or any mixture becomes a purée by pushing through a sieve or strainer, or blending or processing finely. Resulting mixture can be made even finer by pouring or pressing through a sieve or strainer. Food is usually cooked before puréeing, but can be fresh, for example, strawberry purée.

Cooked pumpkin pressed through sieve with wooden spoon forms a purée.

Strawberry purée is pressed through a sieve to remove seeds.

MASHING
To mash potatoes or any similar vegetable, it is important to have the vegetable cooked until tender, then drained well. If you want to add butter, add it to the pan, then add milk a little at a time until the desired consistency is reached.

Use a fork or potato masher to crush the vegetable, then continue to mix the vegetable with either a masher or a wooden spoon. Do not process vegetables instead of mashing because they just break down and become mushy.

TOASTING
Nuts and coconut can be toasted by several methods; these are our favourites. They don't need butter; the natural oils do the browning for you. After toasting, remove immediately from tray or pan to cool to room temperature.

To toast nuts: Spread nuts on oven tray, bake in moderate oven for 5 minutes or until lightly browned.

To toast coconut: Place coconut in heavy-based frying pan, stir constantly over medium heat until coconut is lightly and evenly browned.

TO MELT CHOCOLATE
Place chopped chocolate in top half of double saucepan or in heatproof bowl over a saucepan of simmering water. Water in lower saucepan must not touch base of top saucepan or bowl. Do not stir until chocolate is almost melted. It is important not to let water near the chocolate or it will be ruined. Just a drop or two is the danger; a larger amount of water or other liquid is often incorporated, follow individual recipes.

BAKING BLIND

This process is used to cook pastry cases (both sweet and savoury) before filling, to minimise soggy bases on pies and tarts. There are 2 methods we use.

1. Used mainly when a cold cooked filling is spread into the cooked pastry case. Such a filling sometimes has a crumble or meringue topping, which requires only a short browning time in the oven.

Simply prick pastry well all over with a fork; do not prick right through to the base. If an air bubble occurs in the first 5 minutes of cooking time, pierce with a fork or skewer to deflate it.

Follow individual recipes for cooking times, but cases and bases treated like this will take somewhere between 10 and 20 minutes to cook, usually in a moderately hot oven.

2. Cover pastry case with a sheet of greaseproof paper (not waxed) or baking paper, fill the hollow with dried beans, peas or rice. Place the whole thing on an oven tray for easy handling. Bake in moderately hot oven (unless otherwise directed) for 7 to 10 minutes, depending on size and thickness of pastry case.

3. Remove paper and beans from case. The pastry should look a bit leathery at this stage. Return pastry case to oven and bake for further 7 to 10 minutes or until it is cooked through and lightly browned. Pastry case is usually cooled to room temperature before filling.

Allow beans, peas or rice to cool completely, then store in airtight jar for the future use of "baking blind". They cannot be used for any other purpose.

TO COOK RICE

Rice increases in bulk when it is cooked. White rice triples in bulk; brown rice just more than doubles in bulk.

You will need to boil or steam 1 cup white rice to get 3 cups cooked rice, and 1 cup brown rice to get about 2½ cups cooked rice.

The time the rice takes to cook depends on the type used. There are several varieties available which have been treated so they cook in less than 10 minutes. The ordinary short grain and long grain white rice will take between 10 and 15 minutes. Brown rice will take from 25 to 30 minutes, depending on how crunchy you like it; some people like to cook it even longer.

Rice can be cooked in the microwave oven (see instructions right) but it takes about the same time as for boiled rice.

Rice can be boiled or steamed up to 4 days ahead; keep, covered, in refrigerator. Rice can be frozen for up to 2 months. It can be thawed in a microwave oven; the time will depend on the quantity. Check the manufacturer's instructions.

Here are the 2 main methods of cooking rice.

To boil rice: Two-thirds fill large saucepan or small boiler with hot water. Cover pan, bring to boil, gradually add rice to the water (if you drop it in all at once the water will go off the boil because of the temperature drop and the rice will stick to base of pan and be gluggy).

Boil rice rapidly, uncovered, until just tender. Do not over-cook rice.

After rice is cooked, tip it into a large strainer or colander and drain it well.

If you want to use it cold, for example, for a salad or in fried rice, spread it out on absorbent paper or tea-towel to dry and drain thoroughly.

To steam rice: (absorption method): Place rice in strainer or colander, wash well under cold running water.

Choose medium heavy-based saucepan for cooking 1 to 2 cups of rice; a larger pan for more rice, remembering that it increases in bulk.

Place washed rice in pan with a little salt, if you like. Add enough cold water to cover the surface of rice to a depth of 1cm. Place tight-fitting lid on pan, cook over high heat until rice mixture comes to the boil.

Reduce heat to lowest setting, leave covered for about 30 minutes or until the rice has absorbed the water and is tender. Don't check too often as you are letting the steam escape, not cooking the rice.

This method of steaming rice is the same when using manual or electric rice cookers. Check manufacturer's directions.

MICROWAVE COOKING OF RICE

Rice, as a rule, needs double the amount of water to rice; however, 1 cup brown rice needs 2½ cups water. White rice takes about 15 minutes to cook; brown rice about 25 minutes. Use a large shallow dish about 4cm deep for best results. Do not cover rice while cooking, but do stir at least twice during cooking.

TO COOK PASTA

When cooking pasta (macaroni and noodles too), choose a large saucepan or small boiler, two-thirds fill pan with hot water, cover, bring to boil on high heat. Add a teaspoon of butter or oil to the water to help stop pasta boiling over. Add salt, if you like.

Add pasta gradually to pan of rapidly boiling water, boil rapidly, uncovered, until pasta is just tender (al dente).

Drain immediately into strainer or colander, then use as directed. It should not be necessary to rinse pasta under water if it is cooked correctly.

Cooking time varies depending on the freshness of the pasta.

Fresh pasta will take about 3 minutes to cook. Frozen pasta takes a little longer. Dried packaged pasta takes up to about 15 minutes, depending on its size and age.

All these times are estimated after the water comes to the boil.

MICROWAVE COOKING OF PASTA

Cooking time for pasta will vary depending on the heat of the water and type of pasta used. Fresh pasta will take the least time to cook; packaged pasta the longest. Use a large shallow dish about 4cm deep for best results. Do not cover pasta while cooking, but do stir at least twice during the cooking time.

COOKING LANGUAGE

We have tried to avoid using technical jargon, but here are some expressions which are used commonly in our publications and will help you to cope with most recipes.

Blanch: Means to drop food into a pan of boiling water. Usually the food is returned to the boil, then drained immediately and often then plunged into iced water to stop the cooking and retain the colour.

Knead: Usually done on a board or bench. It means to use the hands to turn the outside edges of mixture into the centre. There are many different reasons for kneading. It can be just to shape the mixture into a smooth ball or it can be to alter the nature of the mixture by working it with your hands.

Marinade: This is a mixture in which food is stood or soaked for anywhere between 20 minutes and 2 days. The reasons are to impart the flavour of the marinade into the food and sometimes to tenderise. This process is called marinating.

Boil: This stage is when the surface of the water is bubbling all over. The temperature is 100 degrees Celsius (212 degrees Fahrenheit). If a recipe calls for a liquid to be brought "up to the boil", this means tiny bubbles appear around the side of the pan at the surface level.

Simmer: This stage is just below boiling point. There should be an odd bubble bursting the surface of the water. The temperature of simmering water is about 88 degrees Celsius (190 degrees Fahrenheit).

Microwave: We used ovens with varying outputs of power between 650 and 700 watts. We have given approximate cooking times to give you a guide, where microwaving is applicable.

APPROXIMATE CUP AND SPOON CONVERSION CHART

Australian	American & British
1 cup	1¼ cups
¾ cup	1 cup
⅔ cup	¾ cup
½ cup	⅔ cup
⅓ cup	½ cup
¼ cup	⅓ cup
2 tablespoons	¼ cup
1 tablespoon	3 teaspoons

OVEN TEMPERATURES

Electric Temperatures	Celsius	Fahrenheit	Gas Temperatures	Celsius	Fahrenheit
Very slow	120	250	Very slow	120	250
Slow	150	300	Slow	150	300
Moderately slow	160-180	325-350	Moderately slow	160	325
Moderate	180-200	375-400	Moderate	180	350
Moderately hot	210-230	425-450	Moderately hot	190	375
Hot	240-250	475-500	Hot	200	400
Very hot	260	525-550	Very hot	230	450

CUP AND SPOON MEASURES

Recipes in this book use this standard metric equipment approved by the Australian Standards Association:
(a) 250 millilitre cup for measuring liquids. A litre jug (capacity 4 cups) is also available.
(b) a graduated set of cups — measuring 1 cup, half, third and quarter cup — for items such as flour, sugar, etc. When measuring in these fractional cups, level off at the brim.
(c) a graduated set of four spoons: tablespoon (20 millilitre liquid capacity), teaspoon (5 millilitre), half and quarter teaspoons. The Australian, British and American teaspoon each has 5ml capacity.

All spoon measurements are level.
Note: We have used large eggs with an average weight of 61g each in all recipes.

GLOSSARY

Some terms, names and alternatives are included here to help everyone use our recipes perfectly.

BACON: rashers are bacon slices.
BREADCRUMBS:
Stale: use 1 or 2 day old white or wholemeal bread made into crumbs by grating, blending or processing.
Packaged: use commercially packaged breadcrumbs.
BEEF:
Eye fillet: tenderloin.
Mince: ground beef.
BISCUIT CRUMBS, SWEET: use any plain, sweet biscuits (cookies). Blend or process biscuits until finely and evenly crushed. Or place biscuits in plastic bag and crush with rolling pin.
BICARBONATE OF SODA: baking soda, a component of baking powder.
BUTTER: we used salted (sweet) butter unless otherwise specified; a good quality cooking margarine can be used;
1 stick butter = 125g butter.
BUTTERMILK: the liquid left from the milk from which cream was made. It is now made by adding culture to skim milk to give a slightly acid flavour; skim milk can be substituted, if preferred.
CHEESE: .
Cottage cheese: we used low-fat cottage cheese with less than 4 percent fat content.
Fetta cheese: we used cheese with about 15 percent fat content.
Mozzarella cheese: we used cheese with about 25 percent fat content.
Parmesan cheese: we used cheese with about 30 percent fat content.
Ricotta cheese: we used cheese with about 10 percent fat content.
Tasty cheese: use a firm, good-tasting cheese. We used cheese which contained about 33 percent fat content.
CHICKEN: numbers indicate the weight, for example: No. 13 chicken weighs 1.3kg. This applies to all poultry.
Breast fillets: skinless and boneless.
Breast on the bone: sold either whole or as half breasts, usually with skin.
Drumsticks: legs with skin intact.
Marylands: joined legs and thighs with skin.
Thigh fillets: skinless and boneless.
CHILLIES, FRESH: are available in many different types and sizes. The small ones (bird's eye or bird peppers) are the hottest. Use tight-fitting gloves when handling and chopping fresh chillies as they can burn your skin. The seeds are the hottest part of the chillies, so remove them if you want to reduce the heat.
CHILLI SAUCE: many varieties available; only trial and error will tell you how much to use. Start with less than a teaspoon; add more if required.
CORNFLOUR: cornstarch.
CREAM: we have specified thickened (whipping) cream when necessary in recipes; cream is simply a light pouring cream, also known as half 'n' half.

Sour: we used a thick commercially cultured soured cream.
Light sour: a less dense commercially cultured soured cream.
CURRY POWDER: a convenient combination of spices in powdered form. In countries where curry is eaten daily, spices are ground individually and combined in endless variations.
   Our recipes tend to be mild in curry flavour rather than hot; the heat can be increased by adding more chilli in the form of sauce or fresh or powdered. Curry powder consists of chilli, coriander, cumin, fennel, fenugreek and turmeric in varying proportions. Buy curry powder in small quantities in airtight containers.
CUSTARD POWDER: pudding mix.
ESSENCE: extract.
FLOUR:
Plain flour: all-purpose flour.
Self-raising flour: substitute plain (all-purpose) flour and baking powder in the proportion of ¾ metric cup plain flour to 2 level metric teaspoons baking powder, sift the mixture together several times before using. If using an 8oz measuring cup, use 1 cup plain flour to 2 level metric teaspoons baking powder.
FRESH GINGER: ginger root.
FRUIT MINCE: mincemeat used in pies, etc, at Christmas or as required.
GHERKIN: cornichon.
GOLDEN SYRUP: maple/pancake syrup. Honey can be substituted.
GREEN SHALLOTS: also known as spring onions or scallions.
GRILL, GRILLER: broil, broiler.
HERBS: we have specified when to use fresh or dried herbs. We used dried (not ground) herbs in the proportion of 1:4 for fresh herbs; for example, 1 teaspoon dried herbs instead of 4 teaspoons (1 tablespoon) chopped fresh herbs.
KUMARA: a variety of sweet potato, orange in colour.
LAMINGTON PAN: a rectangular slab pan with a depth of about 4cm.
MILK: we used homogenised milk (unless otherwise specified) in recipes throughout this book.
MIXED FRUIT: a combination of sultanas, raisins, currants, mixed peel and cherries.
MIXED PEEL: a mixture of chopped crystallised citrus peel.
MIXED SPICE: a finely ground combination of spices which includes allspice, nutmeg and cinnamon; it is used as an ingredient in sweet recipes.
MUESLI: crunchy granola.
MUSTARD, SEEDED: a French style of mustard with crushed mustard seeds.
OIL: use a light polyunsaturated salad oil.
OYSTER SAUCE: a rich brown sauce made from

oysters cooked in salt and soy sauce, then thickened with different starches.
PEPPERS: capsicum or bell peppers.
PUNNET: basket holding about 250g fruit.
RED CURRANT JELLY: a preserve made from red currants; it is an imported product available from some supermarkets and delicatessens.
SCONES: baking powder biscuits.
SESAME OIL: made from roasted, crushed white sesame seeds, is an aromatic golden-coloured oil with a nutty flavour. It is always used in small quantities. It is not the same as the sesame oil sold in health food stores and should not be used to fry food. It is a flavouring and can be bought in supermarkets and Asian food stores.
SMALL STOCK CUBE: equivalent to 1 teaspoon powdered bouillon.
SNOW PEAS: also known as mange tout, sugar peas or Chinese peas, they are small flat pods with barely formed peas; they are eaten whole. You need only to top and tail young pods, older ones need stringing. Cook for a short time (about 30 seconds) either by stir-frying or blanching, or until tender-crisp.
SOY SAUCE: fermented soy beans are the basis for this extensively used sauce. We use 2 types of soy sauce. The light sauce is generally used with white meat dishes, and the darker variety with red meat dishes but this is only a guide; the dark soy is generally used for colour and the light for flavour. There is a multi-purpose salt-reduced soy sauce available. It is a matter of personal taste which sauce you use.
SPINACH:
English spinach: a soft-leafed vegetable, more delicate in taste than silverbeet (spinach); however, young silverbeet can be substituted for English spinach.
Silverbeet: a large-leafed vegetable; remove white stalk before cooking.
SUGAR: we used a coarse granulated table sugar unless otherwise stated.
Castor: fine granulated table sugar.
Brown: soft brown sugar.
Icing: confectioners', or powdered sugar. We used the icing sugar mixture, not pure icing sugar.
Raw: natural light granulated sugar.
SULTANAS: seedless white raisins.
TOMATO PUREE: known as tomato sauce in some other countries. You can use canned tomato purée or a purée of fresh, ripe tomatoes made by blending or processing the amount for the recipe.
TOMATO SAUCE: tomato ketchup.
WHITE FISH: simply means non-oily fish. We used varieties such as bream, flathead, whiting, snapper, jewfish and ling.
WHOLEMEAL: wholewheat.
YOGHURT: we used low-fat plain yoghurt with about 0.2 percent fat content.
ZUCCHINI: courgette.

INDEX

A

Anzac Biscuits	116
Apple and Dried Fruit Crumble	97
Apple Pie, Old-Fashioned	86
Apple Sauce, Roast Pork with	36
Apples, Creamed Rice with Stewed	81
Avocado and Grapefruit Cocktail, Prawn	10

B

Bacon and Fresh Herb Muffins	106
Baked Custard	91
Baked Dinner	40
Baked Fish Cutlets, Oven-	13
Baked Honeyed Chicken Wings, Oven-	57
Baked in Foil, Fish	13
Baked Lamb Dinner with Vegetables	41
Baked Rice Custard	90
Basic Butter Cake	111
Basic Muffins with Apricots	106
Basic Pikelets	89
Basic Rock Cakes	113
Basic Scones	108
Basil Mayonnaise, Chicken Breasts with	54
Bean Salad, Quick	68
Beef and Vegetable Soup, Hearty	71
Beef in Red Wine Casserole	20
Beef Stroganoff	22
Berry Cream Soufflés	98
Birthday Sponge	114
Biscuits, Anzac	116
Boiled Eggs	5
Bolognese Sauce	75
Brains, Fried Crumbed	44
Brains, Lambs'	44
Bread and Butter Custard	91
Burger, Fried Egg	8
Butter Cake, Basic	111
Butterfly Pork Steaks with Two Sauces	34

C

Cake, Basic Butter	111
Cake, Lime Streusel Coconut	112
Casserole, Beef in Red Wine	20
Casserole, Chicken and French Onion	52
Casserole of Veal and Tomatoes	27
Casserole, Rabbit and Bacon	63
Chicken and Corn Soup	74
Chicken and French Onion Casserole	52
Chicken and Vegetable Stir-Fry, Chilli	60
Chicken and Yoghurt Drumsticks	58
Chicken Breasts with Basil Mayonnaise	54
Chicken Liver Pâté with Port	62
Chicken 'n' Chips	50
Chicken Satay with Peanut Sauce	59
Chicken, Seasoned Roast	50
Chicken Wings, Oven-Baked Honeyed	57
Chicken with Green Peppercorn Sauce, Pan-Fried	56
Chicken with Tomato Bacon Sauce, Pan-Fried	61
Chilli Chicken and Vegetable Stir-Fry	60
Chips, Chicken 'n'	50
Chocolate Apricot Ring, Frosted	111
Chocolate Mousse, Easy Rich	104
Chocolate Self-Saucing Puddings	96
Chocolate Slice	119
Cinnamon Teacake	107
Cocktail, Prawn, Avocado and Grapefruit	10
Coconut Lime Streusel Cake	112
Coconut Slice, Raspberry	118
Cold Soufflés	98
Coleslaw	66
Compote, Dried Fruit	4
Compote in Lemon Ginger Syrup, Fruit	4
Cookies, Cornflake Sultana	116
Cornflake Sultana Cookies	116
Corn Soup, Chicken and	74
Creamed Rice with Stewed Apples	81
Creamy Ham and Mushroom Sauce	77
Crème Caramel	92
Crisp Coleslaw	66
Crumbed Fried Brains	44
Crumbed Marinated Lamb Cutlets	48
Crumble, Apple and Dried Fruit	97
Curried Eggs	5
Curried Lamb, Quick	46
Curried Pasta Salad	69
Curry, Easy Lamb and Tomato	46
Custard, Baked	91
Custard, Baked Rice	90
Custard, Bread and Butter	91
Custard, Stirred	102
Cutlets, Crumbed Marinated Lamb	48

D

Dried Fruit Compote	4
Drumsticks, Chicken and Yoghurt	58

E

Easy Baked Slice	118
Easy Fried Rice	79
Easy Lamb and Tomato Curry	46
Easy Rich Chocolate Mousse	104
Egg Burger, Fried	8
Egg, Poached	6
Eggs, Boiled	5
Eggs, Curried	5
Eggs, Herbed Scrambled	7

F

Fig Muffins, Wholemeal	106
Filet Mignon with Mushroom Sauce	24
Fillo Pastry	84
Fish Baked in Foil	13
Fish Cutlets, Oven-Baked	13
Fish, Pan-Frying	12
Fish with Tartare Sauce, Pan-Fried	12
French Dressing, Rice Salad with	68
French Omelette with Ham and Cheese	9
French Onion Casserole, Chicken and	52
Fresh Tomato Soup	73
Fried Brains, Crumbed	44
Fried Egg Burger	8
Fried Fish with Tartare Sauce, Pan-	12
Fried Rice	79
Frosted Chocolate Apricot Ring	111
Fruit Compote, Dried	4
Fruit Compote in Lemon Ginger Syrup	4
Fruit Crumble, Apple and Dried	97

G

Grapefruit Cocktail, Prawn, Avocado and	10
Grilled Kidneys with Red Currant Sauce	45
Grilled T-Bone Steak with Three Butters	26

H

Ham and Mushroom Sauce, Creamy	77
Healthy High-Fibre Muesli	4
Hearty Beef and Vegetable Soup	71
Herbed Scrambled Eggs	7
Honeyed Chicken Wings, Oven-Baked	57

K

Kidneys, Lambs'	45
Kidneys with Red Currant Sauce, Grilled	45

L

Lamb and Tomato Curry, Easy	46
Lamb Cutlets, Crumbed Marinated	48

INDEX

Lamb Dinner with Vegetables, Baked 41
Lamb, Quick Curried 46
Lambs' Brains 44
Lamb's Fry with Bacon 43
Lambs' Kidneys 45
Lamb with Sweet Garlic and Herb Crust, Racks of 39
Lemon Delicious, Light 'n' Luscious 95
Light 'n' Luscious Lemon Delicious 95
Liver Pâté with Port, Chicken 62

M

Macaroni Cheese 78
Marshmallow Pavlova 100
Mayonnaise, Waldorf Salad with Home-Made 70
Meatloaf, Tasty Baked 17
Melting Moments 116
Meringue 100
Mornay Sauce 16
Mornay, Tuna 16
Mousse, Easy Rich Chocolate 104
Muesli, Healthy High-Fibre 4
Muffins, Bacon and Fresh Herb 106
Muffins, Wholemeal Fig 106
Muffins with Apricots, Basic 106
Mushroom Sauce, Creamy Ham and 77
Mushroom Sauce, Filet Mignon with 24
Mushroom Sauce, Tasty Herbed Rissoles with 18

O

Old-Fashioned Apple Pie 86
Omelette with Ham and Cheese, French 9
Oven-Bag Cooking 63
Oven-Baked Fish Cutlets 13
Oven-Baked Honeyed Chicken Wings 57

P

Pancakes with Lemon and Sugar 88
Pan-Fried Chicken with Green Peppercorn Sauce 56
Pan-Fried Chicken with Tomato Bacon Sauce 61
Pan-Fried Fish with Tartare Sauce 12
Pan-Frying Fish 12
Pasta Salad, Curried 69
Pastry, Fillo 84
Pastry, Rich Shortcrust 82
Pastry, Simple Sweet 86
Pâté with Port, Chicken Liver 62
Patties, Salmon 14
Pavlova, Marshmallow 100
Peanut Sauce, Chicken Satay with 59
Pesto Sauce 76
Pie, Old-Fashioned Apple 86
Pikelets, Basic 89
Pineapple Upside-Down Cake with Stirred Custard 102

Poached Chicken 54
Poached Egg 6
Pork Fillets in Apricot Mango Sauce 31
Pork Steaks with Two Sauces, Butterfly 34
Pork, Sweet and Sour 32
Pork with Apple Sauce, Roast 36
Potato Salad with Egg and Shallots 67
Prawn, Avocado and Grapefruit Cocktail 10
Prawn Cocktail 10
Puddings, Chocolate Self-Saucing 96
Pumpkin and Ginger Loaf 111
Pumpkin Cream Soup 72

Q

Quiche Lorraine 82
Quick Bean Salad 68
Quick Curried Lamb 46

R

Rabbit and Bacon Casserole 63
Racks of Lamb with Sweet Garlic and Herb Crust 39
Raspberry Coconut Slice 118
Red Wine Casserole, Beef in 20
Red Wine Sauce, Tomato with 76
Rice Custard, Baked 90
Rice, Easy Fried 79
Rice, Fried 79
Rice Salad with French Dressing 68
Rice with Stewed Apples, Creamed 81
Rich Shortcrust Pastry 82
Risotto, Tomato 80
Rissoles with Mushroom Sauce, Tasty Herbed 18
Roast Chicken, Seasoned 50
Roast Loin of Pork 36
Roast Pork with Apple Sauce 36
Rock Cakes, Basic 113

S

Salad, Curried Pasta 69
Salad, Quick Bean 68
Salad with Egg and Shallots, Potato 67
Salad with French Dressing, Rice 68
Salad with Home-Made Mayonnaise, Waldorf 70
Salmon Patties 14
Satay with Peanut Sauce, Chicken 59
Sauce, Bolognese 75
Sauce, Creamy Ham and Mushroom 77
Sauce, Mornay 16
Sauce, Pesto 76
Sauce, Tomato with Red Wine 76
Schnitzel, Wiener 28
Scones, Basic 108
Scrambled Eggs, Herbed 7
Seasoned Roast Chicken 50
Self-Saucing Puddings, Chocolate 96

Shortcrust Pastry, Rich 82
Simple Sweet Pastry 86
Slice, Chocolate 119
Slice, Easy Baked 118
Slice, Raspberry Coconut 118
Slice, Unbaked 119
Soufflés, Berry Cream 98
Soup, Chicken and Corn 74
Soup, Fresh Tomato 73
Soup, Hearty Beef and Vegetable 71
Soup, Pumpkin Cream 72
Spinach Pie 84
Sponge, Birthday 114
Sponge Cake 114
Steak with Three Butters, Grilled T-Bone 26
Stewed Apples, Creamed Rice with 81
Stir-Fry, Chilli Chicken and Vegetable 60
Stir-Frying 32
Stirred Custard, Pineapple Upside-Down Cake with 102
Stroganoff, Beef 22
Sultana Cookies, Cornflake 116
Sweet and Sour Pork 32

T

Tabbouleh 64
Tartare Sauce, Pan-Fried Fish with 12
Tasty Baked Meatloaf 17
Tasty Herbed Rissoles with Mushroom Sauce 18
Tasty Tabbouleh 64
T-Bone Steak with Three Butters, Grilled 26
Teacake, Cinnamon 107
Toasted Muesli 4
Tomato Risotto 80
Tomato Soup, Fresh 73
Tomato with Red Wine Sauce 76
Trifle 94
Tripe in Parsley Sauce 30
Tuna Mornay 16

U

Unbaked Slice 119
Upside-Down Cake with Stirred Custard, Pineapple 102

V

Veal and Tomatoes, Casserole of 27
Vegetable Soup, Hearty Beef and 71

W

Waldorf Salad with Home-Made Mayonnaise 70
Wholemeal Fig Muffins 106
Wiener Schnitzel 28